D1558907

"After Mecca"

"*After Mecca*"

WOMEN POETS AND THE BLACK ARTS MOVEMENT

CHERYL CLARKE

RUTGERS UNIVERSITY PRESS
New Brunswick, New Jersey, and London

LIBRARY OF CONGRESS CATALOGING-IN-PUBLICATION DATA

Clarke, Cheryl, 1947–
    "After Mecca" : women poets and the Black Arts Movement /
Cheryl Clarke.
        p.   cm.
    Includes bibliographical references and index.
    ISBN 0-8135-3405-4 (alk. paper) — ISBN 0-8135-3406-2 (pbk.)
    1. American poetry—African American authors—History and
criticism.   2. Women and literature—United States—History—
20th century.   3. American poetry—Women authors—History and
criticism.   4. African American women poets—Intellectual life.
5. African American women in literature.   6. African Americans in
literature.   7. Black Arts movement.   I. Title.
    PS310.N4C48 2004
    811'.509896073—dc22

                                                    2004007530

A British Cataloging-in-Publication record for this book is available
                    from the British Library.

Manufactured in the United States of America

To the memories of Lionel Cuffie of Keyport, New Jersey, Eleanor R. Ross of Highland Park, New Jersey, Carol L. Sanchez of Highland Park, New Jersey, and Karen G. Smith of Las Cruces, New Mexico, and Somerset, New Jersey. They were my teachers at crucial times in my life, and I miss my teachers.

CONTENTS

Acknowledgments

I AM DEEPLY grateful to Ms. Nora Brooks Blakely, daughter of the late Gwendolyn Brooks, for allowing me to use "After Mecca," the title of the second part of Ms. Brooks's 1968 volume, *In The Mecca*, as the lead title of this book. At the risk of seeming to make a memoir of this space, anyone who's been in school as many times and as long as I have, has had many teachers. I would like to pay tribute here to some of them. Professors Jean Marie Miller, Carolyn (Taylor) Mitchell, and the late Arthur P. Davis stoked my passion for African-American and U.S. literature during my time as an undergraduate at Howard University from 1965 to 1969. Not being isolated with this passion has been critical. So in 1972, I taught one of the first college courses on black women writers for the Rutgers College English Department called "The Literary Imagination of the Black Woman," which brought me into contact with other feminists and sealed my commitment to the study of black women's writing and black feminist thought. I have enjoyed and still enjoy vigorous conversations about African American literature, most notably with Professors Cheryl Wall, Abena P. A. Busia, and Wesley Brown of Rutgers University, my friends and colleagues for more than twenty-five years. Cheryl and Wesley served on my dissertation committee in 1999–2000, with Cheryl as chairperson. Conversations during 1988 with Professor Mae G. Henderson, of the University of North Carolina at Chapel Hill, still inform my thinking about African American women writers. All these teachers have kept me believing that there is plenty of scholarship still to be done on the writing Africans have wrought in the putative new world.

When I reentered graduate school in 1991, I joined a community of scholars—students and teachers—who made my pursuit of the Ph.D. a communal project. Professors Donald Gibson, Harriet Davidson, Cora Kaplan, Ed Cohen, and Marcellus Blount encouraged my work. Harriet Davidson's seminar, "Poetry and the Post-Modern," in 1992, particularly opened the field of poetry for me. In that seminar I formed invaluable intellectual bonds with my fellow students Kathleen Crown, Nick Yasinski, and especially my brilliant friend, Miriam Bartha. Miriam and I were dissertation partners, met weekly for the 1999–2000 academic year, and shared our work on contemporary poetry and popular culture. We created a space wherein we theorized brazenly about poetry's impact on everyday living since the end of World War II. As we and our country face the aftermaths of our current wars in Afghanistan and Iraq, Miriam and I continue to talk deeply on the unending cultural need for poetry's intervention.

As much as I value the experience of studying for my doctorate, my experience between 1975 and 1990 as a practicing poet, essayist, and editor gave me such fulfillment and joy and the stamina first to produce that unruly thing called a dissertation and then to produce this book. I want to thank Barbara Smith, whom I first met in 1975, for inviting me to a series of black feminist retreats from 1978 to 1980, which introduced me to other black feminists from all over the United States. I also wish to thank Barbara for asking me to write my first book review—of Ntozake Shange's *nappy edges*—for *Conditions: Five, the Black Women's Issue* in 1979 and then in 1981 to write one of my two crucial articles, "The Failure to Transform: Homophobia in the Black Community," for *Home Girls: A Black Feminist Anthology*. Thanks must also go to poet and playwright Cherríe Moraga for asking me in 1979 to write the other of my two crucial articles, "Lesbianism: an act of resistance," for the groundbreaking anthology *This Bridge Called My Back: Writings by Radical Women of Color*. In 1981 also, I was asked by Elly Bulkin, Rima Shore, and Jan Clausen to become one of the eight members of the multicultural editorial collective for *Conditions*, a lesbian-feminist literary journal, founded in 1976. Thanks to them for providing me with such a marvelous learning experience during nine productive years. Because of my work, I was fortunate to have known the late Gwendolyn Brooks, Toni Cade Bambara, Audre Lorde, June Jordan, and Pat Parker. The spirit of each emboldens me still to do my work. From 1977 to 1987, I was fortunate to have had great conversations with Linda C. Powell, who always encouraged my writing and pushed me to self-publish my first book of poetry. My sister, novelist Breena Clarke, also encouraged my writing by staging and directing for public performance my first book of poetry, *Narratives: poems in the tradition of black women*. I want to thank my dear friend of twenty-three years, Evelynn M. Hammonds, whose brilliance I never get enough of, for always including me in her black feminist projects, especially the 1995 conference, "Defending Our Name: Black Women in the Academy," at M.I.T. My writing soulmate, Jewelle L. Gomez, and I traversed this country during the 1980s, reading our poetry and spreading the lesbian-feminist good news. I thank her from the deepest recesses of my heart for her support and friendship over these last twenty-five years. And finally, the profound Barbara Balliet, historian, friend, life partner, and soulmate—with her quick, deep, and encompassing mind—always excites me to do my work by doing hers.

"After Mecca"

Introduction

'AFTER MECCA'

BLACK WOMEN WERE key poets, theorists, and revolutionists during the era of the new black consciousness movement of the late twentieth century, but they had been integral voices since the time when Phillis Wheatley (1774) and Maria M. Stewart (1832) claimed the public and intellectual spheres for African women in North America. However, critical engagement of the poetry of African American women in no way clutters the literary landscapes of either the black or the white West.

Black women poets and fiction writers have worked especially hard since the 1960s to revolutionize the literary terrain of the United States. In *'After Mecca': Women Poets and the Black Arts Movement I* analyze a period of only ten years from 1968 to 1978; however brief, this was an unquestionably generative period in the development of U.S. black women writers, buttressed at the beginning of the decade by Gwendolyn Brooks's *In The Mecca* and at the end by Audre Lorde's *The Black Unicorn*. Black Arts women poets jerked "out of joint" (Brooks, *Broadside Treasury* 37) the consciousness of black Americans as they continued their struggle for radical subject-positioning. The words of women cleaved art and activism, creating dangerous binaries and new possibilities.

This study focuses on black communities struggling first for rights and liberation and their impact on the cultural work of the Black Arts Movement and its production of the new black poetry. The use of the trope "Mecca" resonates with black consciousness movement of the 1960s and 1970s in the United States, a demand to turn away from the (white) West. In turning away, black artists created a new lexicon of prescriptive and proscriptive blackness, which continues to influence the practice of African American culture. Both the Black Arts and Black Power movements were generative of a new political and cultural agency among African Americans. Poetry was a principal instrument of political education about the new blackness. Wherever they stood in relation to the Black Arts Movement, most black women writers of that time wrote *because* of it—and still do.

The experimentalism of the new black poetry, its critique of Western canonical constructions, its revision of African American literary and cultural conventions, and its visionary salience set it apart from the work of the previous generation of black poets. "Mecca," then, comes to represent the struggle of black people, during the late twentieth century, to envision a world in which African American culture occupied the center. This "Mecca" is as much to be struggled toward as struggled for—much like Malcolm X's "hadj" and Martin Luther King's "mountaintop," one is always getting there.

This book takes its title from "'After Mecca,'" the second part of Gwendolyn Brooks's 1968 volume of poetry *In The Mecca*. "'After Mecca'" signifies that time following African Americans' rejection/sacrifice of the possibility of partnership in the American project and their reliance upon the values of the (white) West. During this intense period of social change, African Americans dreamed a different world and imagined a different black community where their rich heritage and culture would be honored; they created a rhetoric and a vernacular that challenged hegemonic and racist White-Anglo-Saxon-Protestant culture.

"Mecca," a trope of deliverance from Western oppression, is also a place of many deaths. Brooks's 1968 epic poem, "In the Mecca," raises the question of who is left to carry on the mourning and the recuperation. The murders of Martin Luther King, who was broadening his political analysis, and both Kennedys, who had given up their hostility to black Civil Rights activism, marked the culminations of nearly a decade of murder and violence that had swept the country during the 1960s as white Southerners and Northerners grappled with the demise of segregation and the contradictions of integration.

The ultrapublic role, the rambunctious orality, and the communal commitments of the poetry of the Black Arts Movement created turbulence on the literary landscape of Afro-America as the equally ultrapublic, unequivocal, and loud calls for "Black Power" created the same tumults on the political landscape. A riveting rhetorical power, a dramatic defection from the codes of black respectability, and a high moral ground of blackness were assumed by many black poets. Indeed, the women poets like Sonia Sanchez, Nikki Giovanni, Carolyn Rodgers, Jayne Cortez, Elouise Loftin, June Jordan, Audre Lorde, and others opened a wider field for black women fiction writers who came to prominence in the 1970s, among them, Toni Cade Bambara, Alice Walker, Toni Morrison, and Gayl Jones. Ntozake Shange, whose "choreopoem" *for colored girls who have considered suicide/when the rainbow is enuff* I discuss in chapter 5, also walked through that space. In fact, one might conclude in this prose-privileging culture, audiences were relieved to read the fiction writers' seemingly more modulated critiques of the racist patriarchy that is U.S. culture. And a resurgent multicultural feminism in the postmodern 1980s demanded the work of black women writers, as well as the writing of all women of color, be read, studied, and taught in literature, women's studies, and black and ethnic studies programs.

Educator, activist, and cultural worker, the late Toni Cade

Bambara created a feminist/womanist space for black women writers in 1970 as the editor of *The Black Woman: An Anthology*. Poems by Sanchez, Giovanni, and Lorde were reprinted there. The impact of Black Arts poetics, the radical communalism of Student Nonviolent Coordinating Committee (SNCC), and the influences of second wave feminism are palpable in this collection. Widely used in black studies and women's studies courses, it became particularly useful to the then-nascent field of black women's studies.

Angela Davis's "Reflections on the Black Woman's Role in the Community of Slaves," first appearing in *The Black Scholar*, caused a stir in black intellectual circles in 1971. Writing from her prison cell and with only secondary sources like Aptheker's *Documentary History of the Negro in America* and his *Negro Slave Rebellions in the United States* available to her, Davis synthesized a narrative that serves to critique the erasures of black women's historic roles in African-American survival. According to Davis, black women slaves in the United States carried their share of the burden of slavery and then some. "It was not her comrade brother against whom [the black slave woman's] incredible strength was directed. She fought alongside her man, accepting or providing guidance according to her talents and the nature of their tasks. She was in no sense an authoritarian figure; neither her domestic role nor her acts of resistance could relegate the man to the shadows. On the contrary, she herself had just been forced to leave behind the shadowy realm of female passivity in order to assume her rightful place beside the insurgent male" (14).

Bound and determined as it is to make the slaves be heterosexual and to assume a prior history of "female passivity" in the homeland, Davis's article is exemplary of the historical recovery that was being brought to bear on black culture during this period. Alice Walker's novel *The Third Life of Grange Copeland* (1970) and her short stories *In Love and Trouble* (1973), Toni Morrison's novels *The Bluest Eye* (1970) and *Sula* (1973), Toni Cade Bambara's short stories *Gorilla, My Love* (1972), Gayl Jones's novels *Corregidora* (1975) and *Eva's Man* (1976), and other works of fiction by black women caused further reevaluations of black women's subjectivity. Early critical response to these compelling works tended to be lukewarm, but their reception by black women readers was nothing less than ecstatic. However, not until 1977, did Barbara Smith's "Towards a Black Feminist Criticism" in *Conditions*, a lesbian-feminist journal and part of the ascendant feminist print movement, create the impetus for a national reappropriation by black feminist critics of black women's writing. After the critically anemic (and politically repressive) 1970s, most full-length studies, edited collections, course readers, journal articles, and anthologies on black women writers began to appear in the 1980s—chiefly on prose and prose writers.[1]

This study offers an analysis of poetry by black women in the United States from 1968 to 1978, a brief but generative period, during which black women exercised much artistic and writing agency. As a poet who claims Black Arts Movement tutelage, I have always been interested in the connection between blackness and feminism. Blackness opened me to poetry in the 1960s, and feminism and lesbianism in the 1970s. This book is an effort to contribute to the field of African-American studies, in which poetry is often overlooked. In chapters 2, 5, and 6, I offer extended readings of Gwendolyn Brooks's "In the Mecca," Ntozake Shange's *for colored girls who have considered suicide when the rainbow is enuf*, and Audre Lorde's *The Black Unicorn*, respectively. All three works chart new linguistic space and signal shifts away from conventional gender, race, sexual, and literary politics in the writing of the period.

Readings of poems by Jayne Cortez, Carolyn Rodgers, Elouise Loftin, Alice Walker, Lucille Clifton, and others occur throughout chapters 3 and 6, which elucidate black women poets' responses to the protocols of the Black Arts Movement. Ntozake Shange's *for colored girls*, as poetry and theater, has always appealed to me because of its impact on the feminist consciousness of black women; the work enabled many of us to tell a "black girl's story."

Chapter 3, devoted to the Black Arts Movement, is crucial to my argument in chapter 5, which connects Black Arts Movement literacies with black lesbian feminist writing and constructs Lorde's *The Black Unicorn* as the vessel that channels the confluence of black, feminist, and sexual poetics. This final chapter, like Lorde, looks ahead and looks back, as if to acknowledge that the last word is never said.

My years as a practicing poet animate my study of black women's poetry in *'After Mecca'* and continue to animate my commitment to the study of African American poetry. I can only hope my readings of the texts cause more work to be done in this abundant and generous field. Many influenced the writing of this book, not least of all the poets, whose contributions I can only hope to magnify.

CHAPTER 1

'Missed Love'

BLACK POWER AND BLACK POETRY

A STRONG READER of sacred and secular black culture since her childhood in the Detroit of the late 1940s and early 1950s, the prodigious Aretha Franklin could always change the mood and tone of a song, exposing the layers of subtext, and render sublime, sensual, or seamy words the listener/reader hears everyday. She presents her righteous reading of "The Thrill Is Gone" (Rick Darnell and Roy Hawkins 1969) from her 1970 album, *Spirit In The Dark*, which gossipy British music critic, David Nathan, in his liner notes accompanying the compact disk, speculates is Franklin's "swan song to her ex-husband, Ted White."

Franklin *does* infuse the song with "an intensity seldom equaled" (Nathan), but Franklin's failed marital relationship does not *cause* her to sing well. After all, Franklin, born in 1942, had been singing, performing, and recording professionally since she was fourteen years old. Perhaps her interpretation of "The Thrill Is Gone" has everything to do with her ability to read the times and infuse the song with *that* reading. Can we possibly read her cover of this B. B. King hit, recorded only two months before Franklin's, as an elegy, a meditation on loss, a cautionary blues telling the end of possibility for progressive social and political relationships between black and white Americans. Is she evoking "The Thrill Is Gone" as black people's "swan song" to

white regard and their own faith that white people would fi-
nally embrace them as citizens of the American project?

As for a generation of people, slain civil rights leader Mar-
tin Luther King, Jr., was Franklin's hero—and family friend.
King was murdered by career criminal James Earl Ray, as he
stood with his fellow Southern Christian Leadership Con-
ference associates on the balcony of the Lorraine Motel in
Memphis, Tennessee, on April 4, 1968, during one of his most
troubling campaigns. Finally, the insertion in "The Thrill Is
Gone" of "Free At Last," a riff on the Negro spiritual delivered
by her back-up singers, Almeda Lattimore, Margaret Branch,
and Brenda Bryant, conveys just the opposite of the optimism it
conveyed when King invoked it in his famous "I Have a
Dream" speech. This speech, delivered August 28, 1963, in front
of the Lincoln Memorial at the historic and highly contested
March on Washington, projected a humanistic vision of freedom
that included "All of God's children—black men and white
men, Jews and Gentiles, Catholics and Protestants" joining
hands and singing "in the words of the old Negro spiritual, 'Free
at last, free at last: thank God Almighty, we are free at last.'" This
utterance of strategic exultation sadly was not borne out in
practice. And the policies that resulted from this period of black
struggle came to be thwarted in the conservative climate of the
1970s and 1980s.

In the recording, Franklin's tone of resignation and desola-
tion reflects the mood of the Americans who had struggled to
redress the country's racist structural inequalities. In 1972—five
years after the opening of Lyndon Baines Johnson's "Great Soci-
ety," and two years after the King and Robert F. Kennedy assas-
sinations, Hubert Humphrey's nomination for president by the
Democratic party, and Richard Nixon's defeat of the Demo-
cratic agenda—the United States invaded Cambodia, an aggres-
sion that shocked and further debilitated the Left and antiwar
activists. Another somber and foreboding footnote to the new

decade was the death on March 9 of Ralph Featherstone, former Student Nonviolent Coordinating Committee (SNCC) field secretary and activist in Mississippi. Featherstone was killed on the road to Bel-Air, Maryland, when a bomb exploded in the car he was driving. Many believe the bomb to have been planted by the police; others believe that Featherstone was transporting the bomb himself. Aretha Franklin's tone is sinister and mournful—a dangerous melding. Freed of the obligation and commitment to act peacefully for the constitutional promises of citizenship, the speaker warns the object of her pain that her desire for the fulfillment of those promises is "gone away-ay-ay-ay." Following hard upon the melisma, signaling the historic intimacy and familiarity of the betrayal comes the sarcastic thrust of the endearment, "baby." "The Thrill Is Gone" enunciates a loss of faith and a "deformation of mastery," Houston Baker's notion of assertion "in the face of acknowledged adversaries" (50). Black people were turning the tables on white people, talking themselves into the center, and simultaneously calling and pushing white people *out*, as SNCC had done in 1967.

LeRoi Jones/Amiri Baraka's foundational article, "The Changing Same (R&B and the New Black Music)," posits that Rhythm and Blues' seeming preoccupation with "unrequited, incomplete, obstructed, etc., love" is a cover for a "missed love" that is "exactly reflective of what is the term of love and loving in the Black world of America Twentieth Century" (*Black Music* 190). In 1970, as in 1966 when Jones wrote "The Changing Same," "missed love" was most certainly the deficient democratic reciprocity black Americans were still experiencing—that is, the perpetration of racist policies, customs, and practices as endemic to U.S. culture as the stars and stripes sewn onto the fabric of Old Glory. Aided by the machinations of the FBI and the Mitchell Justice Department, most white Americans had chosen once again to dismiss black Americans rather than to allow their coexistence in equality. Aretha Franklin poetizes and politicizes that missed love; hers is one of many cultural acts of mourning in the post-1968 discursive period.

By 1965, so many contemporary betrayals of the citizenship rights of black people had occurred: in 1963, Medgar Evers was murdered in Mississippi, and the bombing of the 16th Street Baptist Church in Birmingham, Alabama, resulted in the deaths of four young black girls, Addie Mae Collins, Denise McNair, Carole Robertson, and Cynthia Wesley. Through intense partisan deal-making, the Democratic National Convention refused to seat the interracial Mississippi Freedom Democratic Committee's delegation led by the charismatic Fannie Lou Hamer in 1964. Also in 1964, the ghastly murders of James Chaney, Michael Schwerner, and Andrew Goodman in Mississippi depressed the morale of the Civil Rights foot soldiers. The beating death of protester Jimmy Lee Jackson in Marion, Alabama, the shooting death of Viola Liuzzo on the road back from Selma to Montgomery, Alabama, and the Watts riots in Los Angeles marked 1965. In a betrayal of a different sort, the distressing assassination of Malcolm X in February 1965 helped dash fervent hopes of alternative strategies of resistance and international intervention. All these conditions produced a new black poetry and a new black American cultural practice. Like the "out" improvisational shift in jazz as performed by John Coltrane, Ornette Coleman, Pharoah Sanders, Albert Ayler, Sun Ra, and the nationalist expressivity of black theater created by Ed Bullins, LeRoi Jones/Amiri Baraka, N. R. Davidson, Richard Wesley, the poetry and the poetry reading were profoundly instrumental in advancing and prescribing masculinity and heterosexuality. The poetry forecasted and corroborated the radical revisioning of the place of African-Americans in the mind and body politic of the "wite america" (Sanchez," *We A BaddDDD People* 19).

Also in 1965, poet and activist Dudley Randall, founded

the Broadside Press in Detroit and published the work of the growing community of black and black nationalist–identified poets whose words were changing the culture:[1] for example, Nikki Giovanni, Doughtry Long, Marvin X (formerly Jackmon), Don L. Lee, Jon Eckels, Sonia Sanchez, Margaret Danner, Stephany, Lance Jeffers, Etheridge Knight, and Keorapetse Kgositsile. Printed cleanly, plainly, and neatly, Broadside publications were exploding chapbooks of new black significations. That same year, Joe Goncalves in San Francisco established *The Journal of Black Poetry*, which became a West Coast medium of expression for the new black poet as artist. LeRoi Jones/Amiri Baraka established the Black Arts Repertory Theater in Harlem in 1965 as well; he is often credited as the progenitor of the Black Arts Movement. Throughout the rest of the decade, it became clear that the cultural revolution in black letters was a national awakening, not merely a regional phenomenon of East Coast urban centers.

Slightly less than a year later, in 1966 the slogan "Black Power" was championed by SNCC stalwarts Stokely Carmichael and Willie Ricks to the absolute surprise and shock of Martin Luther King, Jr., in Greenwood, Mississippi, in 1966 and engendered a revolutionary change of consciousness in Afro-America. James Meredith, the first black student to attend the University of Mississippi (1961), was shot three times as he tried with four other people to march 226 miles from Memphis, Tennessee, to Greenwood, Mississippi to publicize a voter registration drive and to protest the brutality of state law officials in preventing black Mississippians from voting. Carmichael, King, and Floyd McKissick descended upon Memphis where Meredith had been hospitalized to pressure him to continue the march under the sponsorship of their three organizations, SNCC, Southern Christian Leadership Conference (SCLC), and Congress of Racial Equality (CORE). On the day of a rally to be held in Greenwood, Carmichael and two other SNCC staffers were arrested and held in jail for six hours when they allegedly "defied" a police order not to erect tents on the grounds of the local black school. Later that evening at the rally, in a line-up that included King, McKissick, and Ricks, Carmichael was last to speak. The protesters had already been worked up by Ricks, well-known for his ability to stir an audience, when Carmichael, still angered by his arrest earlier in the day and also quite capable of stirring an audience, told the six hundred people that he was not going to jail "no more." He then urged the audience repeatedly to demand, instead of freedom, "black power." Carmichael initiated a responsive chant with the audience: each time Carmichael called, "Black power!", the audience responded with "Black power!" (Carson 209). Carmichael quickly became a black militant celebrity as chairman of SNCC and a major articulator of the new black political consciousness.[2]

Certainly, 1966 was not the first time African-American people decided to remake themselves *new*. During the New Negro Renaissance (c. 1917–1930), "New" signified a break with the past, with the South, with slavery, a rebirth to embrace modernity and modernism as well as to enunciate to Europeans/Euro-Americans that Africans/African-Americans were just as capable of culture and civil society as they were. The new generation of artists would be seen and cause the race to be seen not as society's wards, but as 'collaborator[s]' and 'participant[s]' in American civilization" (4). However, "new" to the Black Arts writer meant a decided rupture with the "West/a grey hideous space" (Jones 62).

Formally, the African-American literary tradition begins with poetry and poets—not the slave narrative. From the perspective of proponents of the Black Arts Movement, early verse-makers—such as Lucy Terry (early eighteenth century), Jupiter Hammon (1720?–1806?), Phillis Wheatley (1753–1784), George Moses Horton (1797–1883)—were totally bereft of agency, and their art went begging upon comparison with the "hollers, chants, arwhoolies, and ballits" (*Home*, 106) created and sung by blacks enslaved in North America, according to Leroi Jones's notorious 1962 essay, "Myth of a Negro Literature."[3]

Jones's hostile attack on Wheatley's poetry as a "ludicrous departure from the voices that splintered southern nights" is as dismissive as Thomas Jefferson's declaration that Wheatley's poems were "below the dignity of criticism" (140).[4] Jones also echoes Richard Wright's "niggling review" of Zora Neale Hurston's *Their Eyes Were Watching God* in 1937; in that he asserts that this crucial black woman writer's text was merely a "'minstrel technique'" for the enjoyment of white people (Washington 1979, 17). In "A Dark Bag" (1963), also in *Home*, Jones continues his explosions of the so-called myth of a Negro literature, as he lops off the heads of editors of several anthologies, Arna Bontemps's *American Negro Poetry* and Langston Hughes's *Poems from Black Africa* among them, for their amateurish and anemic selections. The reason for their "tasteless breadth of . . . selection" is, of course, owing to the fact "there has not been overly much to anthologize" (125).[5]

In 1965 as well, Jones/Baraka had defined the "Black Artist's" role as "the destruction of America as he knows it" ("State/ meant" 169). The pronoun "he" seems to privilege black men. However, black women heard it and entered the circle as well— and much on their own terms. "Black" as racial/cultural/political signifier of the African world was spoken and written furiously. Poets became the chief transmitters of "Blackness."

The *Journal of Black Poetry*,[6] in the fall of 1967, reported that the poets at the Black Arts Convention of 1967 determined the black artist to be dealing with three dilemmas: "Is he activist or writer; Black or universal; artist or propagandist" (2). One could say that black writers had the responsibility to join each binary, except one, for they were called upon to be activists *and* writers, artists *and* propagandists, but "Black" and not universal. However, upon reflection Gwendolyn Brooks says in her second memoir, *Report from Part Two*: "In the late sixties, [new black poets] tried to do something fresh, defining Black poetry as poetry written 'by Blacks, about Blacks, *to* Blacks'" (96). The preposition "*to*" stands in to critique what Brooks claims is its "wicked" translation to "for." Though she took on the mantle of (black) cultural nationalism during this time, she was not willing to succumb to a separatist relegation of poetry—hers or anybody else's. She continues, "*Any* poetry is FOR *any* readers or listeners willing to investigate it."

Poets of the Black Arts Movement became chief pundits of this new black cultural nationalism. They claimed adherence to four responsibilities, according to the "reportage" of *The Journal of Black Poetry*: "devotion to the struggle," "leadership," "promulgation of the truth," "interpreting to the people what their condition is" (1967, 2). These prescriptions of the Black Arts Movement era were imposed upon recent converts to blackness, much like the codes of "black respectability" were impressed upon recent migrants from the South at the turn of the twentieth century. The rhetoric of the black nationalist intelligentsia, of which poets were card-carrying members, sharply policed the "boundaries of blackness" (Cohen 1997) to its margins.

Negro Digest, part of the mainstream black press, a monthly established in 1950 by pioneering black publisher John H. Johnson and edited by the astute Hoyt W. Fuller, published its annual poetry issue heralding the "Black Aesthetic" in September 1969. "Ameer" Baraka (formerly LeRoi Jones, soon to become Amiri Baraka) wrote the lead article of the same name and claimed, "Our art shd be our selves as self-conscious with a commitment to revolution" (5). In that same issue, Chicago Black Arts poet Carolyn M. Rodgers, in an article entitled "Black Poetry— Where It's At," theorizes upon "the style and subject matter"of the new black poetry. Rodgers's theorizing anticipates the meditations of Henry Louis Gates, Jr., and Houston Baker upon the vernacular sources of African-American critical practice, including resisting binary oppositions. She provides ten categories of African-American linguistic signifiers: "signifying (open, sly, with or about),"[7] "teachin/rappin," "coversoff (rundown, hipto, digup, coatpull)," "spaced/spiritual (mindblower [fantasy], coolout),""bein (self-reflective, upinself, uptight, dealin/swingin)," "love (skin, space [spiritual], cosmic [ancestral]),""shoutin/angry/ cathartic (badmouth, facetoface [warning/confrontation], two faced [irony]),""jazz (riffin, cosmic [Trane], grounded [Lewis])," "du-wah (dittybop, bebop)," and "pyramid (getting us to-gether/building/nationhood)" (8).

I am most intrigued by the undefined and unexemplified "du-wah" and its parenthetical "dittybop, bebop." "Du-wah" or "doo-wop," an idiosyncratic refrain, is an alternate signifier of the Rhythm & Blues (R&B) music of the 1950s. "[D]ittybop" is a 1950s black male urban youth style, a way of dancing or mov-ing rhythmically; and "dittybopper" was applied to those young men, taken with this new black vocal music, who "gathered in stairwells and on street corners everywhere" to harmonize (Bayles 111).[8] And Rodgers draws an important connection be-tween R&B, which emerged in the late 1940s like "bebop,"[9] the improvisational small ensemble jazz playing. Both R&B and bebop, stemming from different roots in the African-American community, broke with previous conventions to create new so-cial, aesthetic, and racial spaces; neither form was particularly hospitable to women.

Perhaps "du-wah" is a cover for the "missed love" Jones/ Baraka speaks of in "The Changing Same," as many of this gen-eration's songs emphasized the difficulty of obtaining love and sex—the lack of reciprocity from the beloved, the often unful-filled sexual desire. If so, one can understand Rodgers's hesita-tion to define it or provide poetic examples in this moment, when the "race" was called upon to be progressive not nostalgic, angry not hurt, manly not weak. Perhaps, one might consider Nikki Giovanni's poem "Nikki Rosa," a critique of the romance

of the "good ole days," as an example of the "du-wah." It ex-
horts white people not ever to have "cause" to write about
black people because they (white people) will "never under-
stand / Black love is Black wealth" (*Black Feeling Black Talk
Black Judgement* 59); that is, white people will miss and misread
the "love" (read "cultural contributions") that could have been
theirs had they not opted for racist exclusion.

Thus, because of its "unprecedented" use by Black Arts
poets, Rodgers devotes "a large amount of discussion to signify-
ing poetry," the primary use of which is "constructive destruc-
tion" (14), that is, to pull the covers off a sister or a brother's
failings in order to get him or her on the revolutionary track, "a
way of saying the truth that hurts with a laugh." The "signify-
ing" category seems to conflate the "teachin-rappin," "cover-
soff," and "shoutin" categories and has, Rodgers claims, "the
power to involve Black people, and to MOVE them" (16). In her
popular "teachin-rappin" poem, "blk/rhetoric," Sonia Sanchez
asks her audience, "who's gonna make all / that beautiful blk /
rhetoric / mean something" (64); she implicitly moves her lis-
teners—that is, her black listeners—to make actual what the
rhetoric theorizes.

By 1970 *Negro Digest* was one of many African-American
institutions to rid itself of the troublesome term, "Negro." *Black
World*, its new name, signaled the change of consciousness
within the black intellectual community. The new black radicals
were urging African-Americans all over the United States to
call themselves "black" with a capital "B." The transformation,
catalyzed by the mass appeal of Carmichael's heartfelt rhetorical
gesture in Greenwood, Mississippi, in 1966, was everywhere ap-
parent in the black world of the United States and had been in
process since the end of World War II. Older black intellectuals
were challenged by their younger counterparts to discover and
recover the diasporic implications of black power. Poets were
dispatched to be, according to Baraka, "creators, and destroyers-

firemakers, / Bomb throwers and takers of heads" ("We are Our Feeling," 6). From Detroit to Chicago to New York to New Orleans to Los Angeles to San Francisco, poets, prime interpreters of and for that intellectual community, left their words on everything from mimeographed sheets produced out of cellars and college organization offices to the slickest trade press publications.

The Black Arts Movement, both regional and national with global implications, was heavily promoted from inside historically black colleges and universities and within the predominantly white institutions that aggressively recruited black students from the late 1960s onward. Little journals flourished during this time of activist and participatory arts and carried the "revolutionary" good news in poetry, music, and theater. Theater, a crucial venue, became instrumental—as never before—in "explaining the people's condition to them." Unlike the imagined "Harlem" Renaissance, the Black Arts Movement announced itself in urban areas North and South, East and West, with much activity in the Midwest: in Detroit, Broadside Press impressively garnered the poetry of this revolutionary movement of letters, and in Chicago, Third World Press garnered much of the rest. Similarly to the way Motown's mega magnate Berry Gordy saw the vitality of Detroit's black baby-boomer generation—as both producers and consumers—Dudley Randall, ten years later, recognized, produced, promoted, and preserved this autonomous cultural movement, whose central objectives were to practice black American culture, to resist cooptation by the "West," and to make a revolution.

The Black Arts Movement called upon the race to become men in ways that subsumed race. Don L. Lee/Haki Madhubuti was one of the most strident of the Black Arts Movement practitioners and signifiers; he demanded that black people reject "the unclean [white] world, the / polluted space" and "move, into our own, not theirs" (67). In his "teaching-rappin" tour de force, "Blackman/an unfinished history," from his fourth book of poems, *We Walk the Way of the New World* (1970), Lee charts the odyssey of the "blackman" from the Great Migrations to "the new cities" after World War I to the "incendiary" sixties, which "brought us black / at different levels" (22). The elision of "black" and "man" signals the poet's preoccupation with his own notion of their inextricability. Blackness structures manhood and manhood becomes the desired end of blackness. In the first of many poems in Lee's volume the speaker exhorts the monolithic "blackman" to build his own institutions and to create a new man:

> create *man* blackman. . . .
> walk thru the
> world as if You are world itself . . . .
> be an extension of everything beautiful & powerful
> . . . .
> HEY blackman look like
> you'd be named something
> like . . . . *earth, sun*
> or *mountain*.
> Go head, *universe*
> . . . .
> be it,
> blackman. (23)

Black Power advocates in SNCC had put moderate black leaders, the federal government, and white Americans on notice with a new combative rhetoric that not only disrupted black reliance on white involvement and patronage but also rejected the place of nonviolent resistance to racist oppression. SNCC staffers authored a "Position Paper on Black Power," a far-reaching treatise on the urgency of "all-black" leadership to the global connection between "broad masses of black people" and "colonial peoples . . . in Africa . . . and Latin America" (Van Deburg

1997, ed. 122). It stated most pointedly: "If we are to proceed toward true liberation, we must cut ourselves off from white people. We must form our own institutions. . . . Too long have we allowed white people to interpret the importance and meaning of the cultural aspects of our society." And in May 1967, after several months of meetings to decide the issue of white participation in SNCC, the few whites remaining in the organization were expelled (Carson 242).

By 1968, the assassinations of Malcolm X, particularly, and then King and Robert Kennedy within two months of one another, the protracted virulence of Southern racism, and the urban rebellions that punctuated the last six years of the decade further alienated African Americans from white Americans, American institutions, and American values. The Kerner Commission, appointed by Lyndon B. Johnson to study the causes of the urban riots, stated frankly in February of that same year that "Our nation is moving toward two societies, one black, one white—separate and unequal" (Hampton and Fayer, eds. 398).

Poets became translators of the postmodern black American (urban) world; and writers, critics, and readers were all called upon to defrock the existing (white) American literary canon. From 1965 to 1975 more than one hundred anthologies of Afro-American literature were published; all featured poetry exclusively or included poetry with a variety of prose forms.[10] These anthologies were either self-published, published by community centers, political institutions, cultural houses, black college student organizations, black movement presses, or produced by trade presses. This era of cultural flowering was as much new birth as it was a period of "rebirth." Many anthologies included historical writing by contemporary black writers as well as essays, poetry, and fiction of previous generations of black writers. "By, For, and About Black People" were the watchwords of the Movement. According to *Afro-American Poetry and Drama: 1760–1975: A Guide to Information Sources*

(French et al. 143), approximately one thousand books of poetry by black American authors were published between 1946 and 1975, almost twice as many as appeared in all the preceding years of publication by blacks. Approximately 695 were published from 1968 to 1976, and of these, approximately 199 were books of poetry by black women.

In step with this new publishing institution-building, Pulitzer Prize–winning poet, Gwendolyn Brooks, left Harper and Row, her publisher for twenty-five years, for Broadside Press of Detroit in 1968. Brooks marks these new reinventions of blackness in her clever 1970 poem, "Young Africans," with its dedication "for the furious," published in *A Broadside Treasury*, her own edited collection of contemporary black poetry. Still intent upon using the deep resources of poetry, here Brooks marks the giving up of conventional prosodic and poetic devices and the taking on of the new "signifying" poetics. Note Brooks's signature use of rhyme and assonance in the first line, the move to a neologism, "poemhood," which takes up the second line, playing on the rhetoric of black camaraderie that mandated a disruption of modernist balance and aloofness:

> Blacktime is time for chimeful
> poemhood
> but they decree a
> a jagged chiming now.
> If there are flowers flowers
> must come out to the road. Rowdy! (37)

The new poetry spoke to black Americans' righteous anger at white Americans, yes! And much of it spoke to new anxieties, interior energies, and soul quests enabled by the new consciousness, as some titles of individual poetry collections insist: for example, Nathaniel Ali Shabazz's *Excerpts from the Diary of a Young Black Slowly Going Mad* (1970), Jayne Cortez's *Pisstained Stairs and the Monkeyman's Wares* (1969), Richard Bailey's *Soul*

Blood Poems (1969), Carolyn Rodgers's *Paper Soul* (1968), Lorenzo Neil Buford's *Men Don't Cry* (1972), Mari Evans's *I Am A Black Woman* (1970), Stephany's *Moving Deep* (1969). Poets were in the streets *reading* white people, "backsliding negroes," and bankrupt Western values. In looking back on the era of the Black Arts Movement, Houston Baker comments in his essay, "Generational Shifts and the Recent Criticism of Afro-American Literature":

> After the arrests, bombings, and assassinations that comprised the white South's reaction to nonviolent, direct-action protests by hundreds of thousands of civil rights workers from the late fifties to the mid sixties, it was difficult for even the most committed optimist to feel that integration was an impending American social reality. Rather than searching for documentary evidence and the indelible faith necessary to argue for an undemonstrated American egalitarianism, the emerging generation set itself the task of analyzing the nature, aims, ends, and arts of those hundreds of thousands of their own people who were assaulting America's manifest structures of exclusion. (Mitchell, ed. 286)

Black writers in America—poets, fiction writers, playwrights, critics, and journalists—were confronted with the wounding of their reputations if they did not begin to use their public voices to address "the nature, aims, ends, and arts" of the black world. Some, like Robert Hayden (1913–1982),[11] who resisted the call to a Black Aesthetic, were publicly scorned by its proponents. Others, and most notably, Gwendolyn Brooks, who opened herself to the challenge of the new literacy, enlisted in this cultural revolution, but not without sorrow.

CHAPTER 2

The Loss of Lyric Space
in Gwendolyn Brooks's
"In the Mecca"

Then
Ask me why I don't write joyous verses
On childhood rambles; odes to tenderness
Politely touched with bearable nostalgia
For little loves and little pains and
freight trains

All of which are proper in their place
As guns and deadly poems are
For my race.

—Simmons, "The Answer"

We part from all we thought we knew of
love.

—Brooks, "In the Mecca"

BLACK WOMEN, AS participants in the U.S.
black consciousness movement of the 1960s, deployed poetry as
a means to theorize on the state of "the race" and "the revolu-
tion"; cleared a larger space for black women writers who
would, in the 1970s, do the work of radically expanding and
redefining the American literary canon with a multitude of dis-
cursive, subversive projects that positioned black women as sub-

jects.[1] My narrative of black women's work sees 1968 as a par-
ticularly productive period of tragedy and regeneration. I dis-
cuss Gwendolyn Brooks's eight hundred-line elegy, "In the
Mecca," which constitutes the first part of her 1968 volume *In
The Mecca*; In chapter 3 I discuss the second part, "After Mecca."

"In the Mecca" mourns the putatively necessary rejection
of Western forms as artistic and cultural prerogatives for black
writers. "Not the pet bird of poets, that sweetest sonnet/shall
straddle the whirlwind" warns the oracular speaker in Brooks's
"Second Sermon on the Warpland" (52). In this line, the sonnet
functions literally and synecdochally for the (white) West. Al-
though Brooks conceived of "In the Mecca" in the early 1950s,
its publication in 1968 marks a culmination of turbulent events
in U.S. culture and politics and black people's role both within
and outside that turbulence. She was neither the first nor the
only black woman poet to voice the new concerns of "the
race," however. The first books of five other significant black
women poets were also published that year: the Broadside press
publications of Audre Lorde's *First Cities*, Nikki Giovanni's *Black
Feeling, Black Talk*, Third World Press's publication of Carolyn
Rodgers's *Paper Soul*, and Harcourt, Brace, Jovanovich's publica-
tion of Alice Walker's *Once*. New York City poet, Sonia Sanchez,
published her first book, *Homecoming*, in 1968 as well. Brooks's
volume, particularly "In the Mecca," richly forecasts the discur-
sive space of black women's poetry in postmodernity.

Gwendolyn Brooks's entire body of work is a life study of
African-American subjectivity, oral and written traditions,
sources of knowledge and faith systems; of the psychic and
emotional effects of racism on the lives of black (and white)
people; and of the richness of the lyric. Brooks wants to come
to terms with giving up the lyric to take poetry from the rar-
efied air of Afro-American modernism to the rarefied air of
black nationalism. For Brooks, the lyric, once her "pet bird,"
functions in "In the Mecca" as the instrument of mourning and

symbol of that which is mourned. As an ancient purveyor of the human condition, the lyric often expresses that "missed love" Jones talks about and the missed meanings of living. Depending upon who deploys it, lyric is both convention and subversion. African-American poets have deployed lyric forms and adapted them to their experiences of "missed love" within American society. No place has lyric invention and reinvention been more expressive than in Rhythm & Blues songs, where unrequited love stands in for the pain of racial exclusion and destruction. Whatever their prosodic variations across continents and ages, lyrics are tied to music, oral traditions, and performance. Brooks is a strong reader of blackness, a strong poet of place and region, which all her life had been the South Side of Chicago; yet she maintained the appropriate modernist distance between self and objects-become-subjects of her gaze—black people.

In The Mecca, Brooks's last book with Harper & Row Publishers, takes its place after a strong line of works that "display the pathos and frustrations of modern life in a restricted neighborhood" (Williams, 58) and marks Brooks's rejection of a "safe" position inside the American literary tradition/canon. Indeed, the Pulitzer Prize winner announced in 1969 that Broadside Press, run by poet and Black Arts Movement promoter, Dudley Randall, would publish her next book, *Riot*.

When *In The Mecca* was published in 1968, that once magnificent Chicago edifice, The Mecca, had been razed for sixteen years. Designed by George Edbrooke, "famous for his ability to utilize aesthetically large spaces," and built by the D.H. Burnham Company in 1891 for the (white) wealthy of Chicago, "The Mecca became one of the early examples of multifamily dwelling." According to Kenny J. Williams: "During the Columbian Exposition of 1893, [The Mecca] was one of the places in the city that visitors wanted to see. (Later it was still a tourist attraction but not because of its beauty.)."

Drake and Cayton in their iconic study of blacks in Chicago, *Black Metropolis*, state that between 1875 and 1893, the year of the Columbian Exposition, the black population in "Midwest Metropolis" (Chicago) tripled, from five thousand to fifteen thousand: "The Black Belt gradually expanded as Negroes took over the homes of white persons who were moving to the more desirable lake-front or to the suburbs. . . . Chicago attracted a large proportion of those who left the South between 1890 and 1910 in what has been called 'the Migration of the Talented Tenth.' . . . By 1910 there were 40,000 Negroes among the heterogeneous two million inhabitants of Midwest Metropolis" (47–53).

The Mecca was girded by three balconies and guarded by ornate wrought iron grillwork. Off these balconies, doors opened to the apartments, "like tiers of cells in a prison cell-block" (Martin 87). John Bartlow Martin wrote about The Mecca for *Harper's Magazine* in 1950, as part of a series on American architectural wonders. In fact, the following excerpt from Martin's lengthy article prefaces the poem, "In the Mecca": "A great grey hulk of brick, four stories high, topped by an ungainly smokestack, ancient and enormous, filling half the block north of Thirty-fourth Street between State and Dearborn" (90).

By 1912, the city's white wealthy had moved to the north (east) side of the city, as the Black Belt again expanded along the South Side, where on State Street, The Mecca now housed Chicago's black elite. The Mecca began its long decline after the Great Black Migrations (1914–1918), World War I (1918), and the Chicago Riot of 1919. By the Great Depression the once elaborate showplace and tourist attraction had become a crowded slum for the black dispossessed and a symbol of encroaching urban blight—a great hulk of modernity confining thousands of expendable people to the bowels of the city.

The Mecca was purchased from a New York estate in 1941 by the Illinois Institute of Technology, whose building was designed by Mies Van de Rohe, to whom Brooks alludes in the second line of "In the Mecca." The Institute wanted to destroy The Mecca from the time it took ownership, but Chicago's political machine prevented that until 1952. In the forties, The Mecca was virtually the only space in which this dispossessed people was allowed to live in segregated Chicago. Better, thought the politicians, that poor blacks be confined to the South Side in The Mecca than to be dispersed all over the city.

The U-shaped Mecca contained 176 units. Some apartments had seven rooms, their hard wood floors were splintered, and beneath their balconies the tile flooring had been broken in many pieces. After the Depression, no one ever knew how many people lived there at any one time: estimates of three thousand to nine thousand people have been given. "'You'll find them sleeping in the kitchen under the sink, anywhere they can sleep,'" one tenant is quoted by Martin in his 1950 article (91).

Brooks began to write *In The Mecca* as a "teenage novel" in 1954 (Melhem 153). She drew upon her firsthand experience as secretary to "a patent medicine purveyor" during the 1940s (Melhem). She had walked through its U-shaped great gray hulk and beyond its littered atria, passed by the once-beautiful marble walls and its once-plush carpeted floors, looked up to see the accumulated dirt and grime on the glass of its skylights emitting a kind of eerie light, passed her hand along its rusted wrought iron railings, and mused over what remained of its nonfunctioning fountains.

Her editors, never enthusiastic about the prose manuscript, counseled that her training in poetry had ill-prepared her for the "freer area of prose" and discouraged her from continuing the project (Melhem). Harper would publish the novella, *Maud Martha* in 1953, the polemical *Beaneaters* in 1960, and the popular *Selected Poems* in 1963, before Brooks turned her attention again to "In the Mecca," this time she conceived the work as a book-length poem, "2,000 lines or more," according to notes she reproduces in her 1972 memoir, *Report from Part One* (189). Her notes also say that she wished "to present a large variety of personalities against a mosaic of daily affairs, recognizing that the *grimmest* of these is likely to have a streak or two streaks of sun."

Brooks came to see the razing of the Mecca building in 1952 as an act of erasure, which by the mid-1960s, was causing her to reconsider her own location and locution in the tradition of African-American writing. In this sense, the poem represents an artistic crisis in her own writing life as she struggled to consider the issues of audience as never before. "In the Mecca" does not recount the elite history of this once palatial dwelling, nor does Brooks inscribe within its narration or its narratives the explicit history of the 1960s. Instead, she allows a collateral story to inhabit the discursive space of its absence. The poem sits as a gate to the entire text of the volume, as if the great gray hulk of the once majestic Mecca, jewel of the Columbia Exhibition, still filled half the block north of Thirty-fourth Street between State and Dearborn.

As "perceptible metaphor and symbol" (Taylor 128), "In the Mecca" is an epic lesson on the spiritual and psychic condition of urban black people in postmodernity, lying in the shadows of "modernity and . . . the Holocaust" and "the social forces of the 1960's" (Wright, ed., Miller 148). The poem honors the sacred and vexed places of language, literacy, and poetry within the culture of black Americans. As elegy, it engages readers in an active wake, a way of mourning, which Philip Novak defines as "a cultivated wakefulness to the poignancy of the present moment in its passing" (189), in his trenchant article on the tropes of death, loss, and mourning in Toni Morrison's *Sula*. That is to say, Brooks invests the texts within the text of the poem with the lyric fortitude that must be sacrificed to "resist the historical trajectory leading toward the extinction of African-American culture" (Novak 191).

Brooks had been captivated by the apocalyptic new black-
ness, first in 1967 in Nashville at the second Fisk University
Writer's Conference where she heard the "militant" younger
poets give new meaning to the act of writing. She wanted a
place among them. In *Report From Part I*, her 1972 memoir,
Brooks describes her precarious status at the legendary confer-
ence as the older generation of writers made way for the "New
Black":

> Coming from white South Dakota State College I arrived
> in Nashville, Tennessee, to give one more 'reading.' But
> blood-boiling surprise was in store for me. First, I was
> aware of a general energy, an electricity, in look, walk,
> speech, *gesture* of the young blackness I saw all about me. I
> had been 'loved' at South Dakota State College. Here I was
> coldly Respected [*sic*]. Here, the heroes included novelist-
> director, John Killens, editors David Llorens and Hoyt
> Fuller, playwright Ron Milner, historians John Henrik
> Clarke and Lerone Bennett . . . Imamu Amiri Baraka, then
> 'LeRoi Jones,' was expected. He arrived in the middle of
> my own offering, and when I called attention to his pres-
> ence there was jubilee in Jubilee Hall. . . . Up against the
> wall, white man! was the substance of the Baraka shout, at
> the evening reading he shared with fierce Ron Milner
> among intoxicating drum-beats, heady incense and organic
> underhumming. Up against the wall! (85)

The drums will do it every time. With zaniness, Brooks ac-
curately reveals the creativity and danger of the baptism-in-
blackness experiences of a generation of black people. (Note:
She only mentions men as heroes.) Brooks felt she could claim
membership in the club, if for no other reason than her dark
skin, because of which many of the "Negro" persuasion had re-
jected her. "Annie Allen," "Maud Martha Brown," "Chocolate
Mabbie," the dark-skinned personas of her pre–Black Arts days,

were foils for her own self-referencing. So, she sought out the tutelage of the "New Black" with much the same spirit as she had entered the poetry workshop run by Inez Cunningham at the South Side Community Art Center in 1941. Brooks was devout about poetry as a vehicle that could teach black people about their history in the world as she herself was being now taught. She says coyly of her position: "I—who have 'gone the gamut' from an almost angry rejection of my dark skin by some of my brainwashed brothers and sisters to a surprised queen-hood in the new black sun—am qualified to enter at least the kindergarten of new consciousness now. New consciousness and trudge-toward-progress. I have hopes for myself" (86).

In some senses the authority of the narrator in "In the Mecca" is at odds with and parallel to Brooks's own subject position as a poet "of new consciousness now" and soon-to-be arbiter of the Black Arts Movement in the Midwest. No longer Hyena, "the striking debutante. / A fancier of firsts" ("In the Mecca" 6), Brooks, the first black person to win a Pulitzer Prize and to be named poet laureate of Illinois, moves her witness out of "her dusty threshold." And like Esu, the androgynous Yoruba god of chance who lurks at gateways, on highways, and at cross-roads (Courlander 10; Gates 29–31), the narrator arrives in the wake of destruction, neither promising nor predicting anything but the further devastation of what was: the annihilation of the actual physical space ironically called "The Mecca," of the humanity of the "dispossessed blacks" who had come to live there and in many urban spaces, and of the relationship with the world outside the Mecca (Williams 60). "Mecca" is, "Boston, New York, Philadelphia, or Los Angeles" (69) as well as Chicago, and all the other urban spaces to which Afro-Americans migrated from the Jim Crow South after World War I. The poem extends a provisional hope—outside "Mecca."

Brooks locates her narrator within a transgressive space and creates a "speakerly text" (Gates, *Signifying* 22), a stage whereupon many speech acts are performed by the narrator as well as by the many subjects of the narration. "In the Mecca" is an enunciation of loss, fragmentation, despair, and death. And the poem is a frantic splitting of the narrative strategies of showing and telling. The text parodies and pays homage to nineteenth-century American narrative, English poetry, black oral traditions, the King James Bible, and the African American synthesis of these, as the narrator warns us, in biblical vernacular, of the Gothic propensities of this telling: "Now the way of the Mecca was on this wise" (4).

The movement of the poem's 807 lines winds narrowly, as if through the corridors of the once splendid dwelling. The reluctant reader, like Mrs. Sallie, the main character and mother of the missing Pepita, is drawn along by the narrator to the inevitable, predictable end. The poem is a text of texts, in which the politics of gender, race, and sexuality are deeply implicated. "In the Mecca" sits as a postmodern elegy on the place of the lyric in African American poetry. LeRoi Jones/Amiri Baraka captures this angry sense of loss in section three of "Rhythm & Blues (I" [sic], a dense, anthemlike poem with expansive lineation, not unlike Allen Ginsburg's "Howl." He dedicates it to the radical civil rights activist, rebel, and exile, Robert Williams:[2] "I am deaf and blind and lost and will not again / sing your quiet / verse" (47).

As much as they signify on antecedent texts, Brooks's strategies of shifting subjectivity, dispersed narration, and polyvocality look forward to the strategies deployed by Toni Morrison in *Beloved.* As the enunciated story/mystery of Sethe's murder of her daughter unfolds, the reader must encounter the slave stories of Paul D., Baby Suggs, Stamp Paid, Sethe's own story, and numerous other liminal and marginal characters whose accounts of atrocities committed against them are as horrific or more horrific than those experienced and committed by Sethe. Morrison, nearly twenty years after the publication of Brooks's visionary work, makes her brilliant, revisionist move in *Beloved*, to critique patriarchal narratives—white and black—of slavery.

The action of Brooks's poem, on the surface, revolves around the search of Mrs. Sallie Smith, for her missing daughter, Pepita, whom she and the reader ultimately discover is murdered. The reader is confronted with a relentless narrator who compels her to hear the stories—in multivoiced and multivernacular irony— of speakers telling their own atrocities, failings, and mysteries framed by a fictional and historical Mecca, infusing the poem with Gothic dread.

Full of temporal inversions, "In the Mecca" functions as mystery and narrative-within-narrative (Gates 209). The modes of narration split sharply between its "showing" of Mrs. Sallie's desperate, yet passive search and the frantic deployment of polyvocal and multidiscourse tellings that split the reader's focus away from Mrs. Sallie's search for Pepita. In each mode of narration, the narrator causes in the reader, crises of witness (Felman 47–48), "an anxiety of fragmentation" (49), a cut-off-ness, an isolation which in the poem is enhanced by the indifference of the other characters/subjects to the fate of the missing child and the distancing, elevated speech acts of the narrator, who, of course, knows the outcome.

Additionally, the play among narrative modes critiques and pays homage to the lyric, the ballad, the sermon, the slave narrative, the proverb, the psalm. The narrator enunciates these strategies, and they are dispersed throughout the modes of discourse adopted by the other telling subjects. Through the deployment of end rhyme, the location of lyric passages, the satirizing of vernacular speech, and the revising of African American storytelling traditions, the poem acknowledges Brooks's "deep and broad familiarity with poetry's technical resources" (Taylor 130) and embraces and extends the formal, metric, and lyric proficiency of her antecedent texts.

Much of what Gates says about Ishmael Reed's *Mumbo*

Jumbo as "a book about texts and a book of texts, a composite narrative composed of subtexts, pre-texts, and narratives-within-narratives" (220), can most certainly be said of "In the Mecca." Each speaker is a text. The narrator functions as Esu, the interpreter of black subjectivity in the poem. The poem is profoundly postmodern in its parodic deployments. Whereas Reed's parodic and mostly male characters set themselves on the odyssey to either destroy or discover "Jes' Grew," the mythic spirit of blackness that is affecting and infecting the white West, Brooks contains her epic sense in the search for a missing girl child, whom no one has seen.

The poem is both telescopic and documentary, evoking hallways, in an almost concrete fashion. The reader, like a reluctant viewer, is directed and commanded to "Sit where the light corrupts your face" (5) and to follow the poem's constricted lineation down the corridors of the place to capture a perverse "social panorama" (Melhem 158). A mediating but unconscious subject led by the narrator, Mrs. Sallie in turn leads the reader through a desolate space ringing with different languages (Jones 195): first as she, home from work, "ascends the sick and influential stair" (5) to her fourth-floor apartment, and then as she winds back through the place in search of Pepita. Ultimately the narrator, without Mrs. Sallie, brings the reader to bear witness to the fact of Pepita's murder, in whose demise the reader may come to reckon with the loss of possibility in the "white West."

At the third line of the poem, "the fair fables fall" (5), the narrator tells the reader that this will be no predictable narrative—not *Annie Allen* and not *Maud Martha*. As quirky as they were, Annie and Maud were the centers. Subjectivity shifts frantically in this poem.

Indirect discourse predominates and functions as the narrator's control of the display of language and the more sympathetic subjects. Direct discourse is allowed more sparingly to evoke humor, sarcasm, realism, irony as well as to underscore the narrator's distance from the enounced. Free indirect discourse is employed to communicate the more authentic historical horrors and the subjects' interiority—and perhaps the narrator's empathy. Christian devotion, as practiced in the Mecca, is called into question through St. Julia Jones's direct and ostentatious expression of religiosity in her farcical exuberance: "'He hunts up the coffee for my cup. / Oh how I love that Lord.'" The narrator retrieves control to show Prophet Williams, the religious charlatan, "rich with Bible" (6), but whose wife Ida "was a skeleton / was a bone," who "died in self-defense" and alone. The narrator's interior eruption, "(Kinswomen! / Kinswomen!)," signifies-on the speaker's appeal in Claude McKay's famous 1919 poem, "If We Must Die," "O, Kinsmen! We must meet the common foe" (Johnson, ed. 169). McKay protests the murders of black men in the bloody summer of race riots in 1919. Brooks laments the sacrifice of black women's lives and bodies, indeed of women's lives and bodies, and signals further sacrifices to be revealed "on this wise." This eruption is perhaps the most explicit expression of gender empathy; and this aside symbolizes the low value placed upon the lives of women. Sexuality, throughout this poem, is configured in male and female subjects as a corrupted (hetero)sexuality.

There is irreparable damage in this place, and Alfred, an unreliable witness whose subjectivity is conveyed primarily indirectly, contends with the narrator for presence. He is much less reluctant than the reader; in persistence, he reappears five times, more than any of the other more than fifty subjects. At times his relationship to the narrator evokes younger black poets' relationship to Brooks; at other times Alfred seems to be a persona for Brooks, preparing to apprentice herself to the younger, "Blacker," (male) Black Arts poets. Alfred has neither the narrator's language nor rhetorical power. He has too many masters and is distracted by too many pretenders: "Shakespeare . . . Joyce or James or Horace, Huxley, Hemingway," "pretty hair," "that golden girl" (7). Aware that his models/mentors will no longer serve him, Alfred relentlessly witnesses and searches for new mentors. Will he be able to take the story out of the Mecca? Or is it a story like Morrison's *Beloved*—not to be retold?

Such hope cannot be extended to Mrs. Sallie and eight of her nine children. The narrator shifts her attention from the reader to "Yvonne," "Melodie Mary," "Cap," "Casey," "Thomas Earl," "Tennessee," "Emmett," "Briggs"—all except Pepita. The children's world is as restricted and dangerous as their names are ambitious and imaginative. Explanatory narratives of impoverishment, sexual exploitation, potential crime and violence, hunger, and isolation interpret each child's psychic and physical space. Yvonne, Mrs. Sallie's oldest, offers a lyric moment of iambic tetrameter as she "prepares for her lover" and a casual and subversive sexuality:

> It is not necessary. . . .
> to have every day him whom
> to the end thereof you will love. (9)

The constriction and cleverness of the lines, underscoring the brevity of Yvonne's encounter, are marvelous examples of Brooks's skillful use of convention to parody the middle-class values of sexual monogamy and permanency. Simultaneously, Mrs. Sallie muses over the space she occupies in two disparate worlds—that of the Mecca where her daughter, "Melodie Mary likes roaches" (10) and that of her "Lady's pink convulsion, toy child . . . under a shiny tended warp of gold" (13). In slant rhyme and sing-song cadence, Mrs. Sallie wishes for a reversal of class and race locations: "'And that would be my baby be my baby. . . . / And I would be my lady I my lady.'"

In vernacular caricature, "'WHERE PEPITA BE?'" Mrs. Sallie asks her daughter's whereabouts, after counting the noses of only seven of her children. However, Pepita is not the only loss or tragedy here: "many flowers start, choke, reach up, / want help, get it, do not get it, / rally, bloom, or die on the wasting vine" (14–15).

Simultaneously paying homage to and parodying the origins of black narrative traditions, Brooks inverts "space and time" by confronting Mrs. Sallie with "Great-great Gram," her first encounter in the search for Pepita (Mootry and Smith, eds., Jones 200). Great-great Gram, seemingly a former slave, renders her testimony, what Gayl Jones refers to as a "(mini) slave narrative," another example of an antecedent text embedded in the surface text. The performative quality of Great-great Gram's narrative is unsettling. Great-great Gram's character feels nearly as parodic as that of St. Julia Jones. However, conveying Great-great Gram's nostalgic yet realistic recollections of slavery through direct address, Brooks connects memory to loss. The missing Pepita does not concern Great-great Gram as much as it stirs memories of slavery, its deprivations, and of her sister, "Pernie May," the dirt floor of "our cabin," and the thing that "creebled in that dirt" (15).

Great-great Gram's memory of her sister is juxtaposed to Mrs. Sallie's missing Pepita, whose name bears metric similarity to the name Pernie May. Great-great Gram's farcical, at turns eloquent enunciation of the slave condition provides some distraction from the terror of the present confronting Mrs. Sallie and the reader: Brooks collapses historical and present time as Great-great Gram's story recalls for the reader the great migrations or *jihads* of the slaves' descendants to the Meccas of the North, like Chicago; and of the historical Mecca building as one of the sites where that history and memory did reside.

Mrs. Sallie's (and the narrator's) next encounter provides another resonant narrative. Loam Norton has not seen Pepita either. He is preoccupied like Great-great Gram, with a correlative atrocity, "Belsen and Dachau." Even the name, "Loam," a composition used in making bricks, signifies the Old Testament story of the Egyptian captivity of the Hebrews; and, as the legend would have it, the Hebrews made the bricks and built the pyramids. Using free indirect discourse for the first time, the narrator enunciates Loam's thoughts (Gates 211), in a cynical revision of another Old Testament text, "Twenty-third Psalm." Brooks only seems to allow direct discourse to certain black speakers, like Great-great Gram. Loam's free indirect discourse also exemplifies the narrator's critical and interpretive control:

> The Lord was their shepherd.
> Yet they did want.
> Joyfully would they have lain in jungles or
> > pastures. . . .
> > > Their gaunt
> souls were not restored, their souls were
> banished. . . .
> Blood was the spillage
> > of cups.
> Goodness and mercy should follow them
> all the days of their death. (15–16)

The past and recent histories of the trans-Atlantic slave trade and the Holocaust of the Jews, respectively, are linked by Loam (and the narrator) through the time-worn signs, "jungles and pastures" (15). Loam's final assertion to the reader, "I am not remote./not unconcerned," vindicates his (and Great-great Gram's) preoccupations with their own grief.

In the article, "'Circles and Circles of Sorrow': In the Wake of Morrison's *Sula*," Phillip Novak speaks about the role of mourning in African American culture and the ways in which Toni Morrison's *Sula*—the text itself—is a "wake," if you will, for the deaths and losses sustained by African people in the so-called New World, that is, "Death presides. And *Sula* endlessly presides over death" (185). The numerous deaths in *Sula* are spectacles for the always already mourning witnesses and metonyms for the "always . . . already gone" (186–187). Great-

great Gram and Loam Norton remind Mrs. Sallie, the narrator, and the reader that the past or death must be "inscribed in our own living on" (186). We must be like "Boontsie De Broe," the next Meccan who has not seen Pepita, "a Lady/among Last Ladies," a vanishing repository of culture, whose race is not clear but whose "clear mind is the extract / of massive literatures, of lores, / transactions of old ocean; suffrages" (16).

Novak's statement that *Sula* presents itself "in the form of an absence" (189) has obvious relevance to "In the Mecca," in its search for the missing Pepita. Brooks, in 1968, and Morrison, in 1972, show us that "to cultivate mourning is to attend to history and at the same time to resist the historical trajectory leading toward the extinction of African-American culture" (191).

The fragmented community of Meccans who do not know "WHERE PEPITA BE" is a meditation on the sacrifices that cause grief, that is, a kind of "cessation of interest in the outside world" (Ramzani 29). To attend to their own histories, all have (and will) relinquish "interest" in the fate of the missing child and their connections to one another.

The reader's hope is not recuperated as she witnesses Mrs. Sallie's encounter with "The Law," represented by two policemen, to whom a missing "Female of the Negro Race" is of less concern than a "paper doll" or a "southern belle" (19). They constrain Mrs. Sallie with the highly symbolic "lariat of questions." The Law leaves. The sinister witness, Aunt Dill, arrives to give false comfort and, within another narrative, forecasts in direct address the accident, the murder of Pepita: "Little gal got / raped and choked to death last week" (19). Aunt Dill's monologue stands as one of the only Afro-American texts, other than slave narratives and contemporary recreations of them, depicting atrocities committed against poor black women. The realistic utterance of such an unreliable witness makes her speech act all the more ironic:

'Her gingham
was tied around her neck and it was red
but had been green before ... and her tongue
was hanging out (a little to the side);
her eye was all a-pop, one was. ... The Officer said
that something not quite right been done that girl.' (18)

Aunt Dill's narrative hardly prepares the reader for one major
crisis of fragmentation in the poem: Mrs. Sallie's discursive
withdrawal from her subject position and from the narrative.
Neither she nor any of her seven children appear again. Accord-
ing to Felman, one's realization of "the dimensions" of the hor-
ror is a process that demands "retreat" (76). Mrs. Sallie and her
seven children leave the narrator and the reader to bear witness
to the outcome (117).

The Law returns, and thus begins the second principal part
of the poem—to ultimately uncover the "accident" (Felman
23). The reader must bear witness to subjects previously en-
countered as well as new ones, even more isolated from one an-
other and more fragmented by their losses and failings.

Alfred appears again to offer a paean, in free indirect dis-
course, to Leopold Senghor, "negritude needing" (20), which
signals movement beyond his own mediocrity, Western deriva-
tiveness, and the lyric: "The line of Leopold is thick with black-
ness/and Scriptural drops and rises" (20).

"The line" refers to the poetic line as much as to the ances-
tral line of Leopold Senghor, the black Senegalese who with
Martiniquan, Aimé Cesaire, and Haitian Léon Damas founded
the Negritude Movement in Paris in the 1930s and from 1960
to 1980 was president of the West African country and former
French colony, Senegal. The last line of the passage quoted above
is a refusal to preserve the sonnet, the "outmoded love" and
heretofore the major repository for Western expressions of

quixotic, quotidian, sexual, and patriotic love. Before "Negritude," Senghor was "rootless and lonely" in Paris, singing in what the narrator calls "art-lines / of Black Woman," paeans of pretty lines to an atavistic loved. Then, as president of Senegal, Senghor's love object changes to nation: "[He] loves sun / listens / to the rich pound in and beneath the black feet of Africa" (21).

Mazola, a new speaker, proclaims herself a witness—not to Pepita's death—but of how easy death is in the Mecca. The lyricality of the passage, an unfinished sonnet, is enhanced by its soft and subtle a-a-a-b-c-c-a-d-e rhyme and the alliteration of its eighth line. Thus, in an indirect mode, the narrator through Mazola laments the loss of the body which represents the death of the lyric in the Afro-American tradition: "the elegant hucksters bearing the body when the body / leaves its late lair the last time leaves. / With no plans for return"(21).

Alfred's paean to Senghor is supplanted by the narrator's competitive praise-song to Don L. Lee/Haki Madhubuti, whose third book of poetry, *Don't Cry, Scream*, is a major articulation of the Black Arts Movement's cultural politics. The proximity of this section to the Senghor section draws attention to the relationship between the Negritude Movement and the Black Arts Movement,[3] both of which called for a reawakening, in those of African descent, to the African essence of blackness and a rejection of Western cultural, especially literary, influences. Brooks had by this time apprenticed herself to Lee/Madhubuti, many years her artistic junior. But his poetry exemplifies the fierceness that forever changed Brooks at the second Black Writers Conference in Nashville in 1967 and, in turn, influenced her writing of *In The Mecca*. So, where Senghor "loves sun," "Don Lee . . . . stands out in the auspices of fire" (21), emphasizing a more dynamic and revolutionary break with the West than Senghor's example of postcolonial accommodation, and makes a more vociferous call for the death of the lyric.

> Don Lee wants
> not a various America.
> Don Lee wants
> a new nation
> under nothing . . . .
> wants
> new art and anthem; will
> want a new music screaming in the sun. (21–22)

This parody of the quotidian declamation, "The Pledge of Allegiance," signifies a turning to new space in the present, the possibility of a new world view and creative production. The Don Lee exhortation may hold out the prospect of reclamation beyond the "art-lines" of Senghor and beyond those of the lyric as well.

The reference to Lee begins to signify more explicitly the black political climate of the 1960s, its radical/revolutionary tenor, the turning of blacks toward themselves and against white sanction, acceptance, tutelage, the violent wrenching of an enduring symbiosis. The arguments between Black Power and Civil Rights advocates—that is, between black nationalism and interracial organizing—frame the poem's first dialogue between Amos and "the gradualist." Amos prays for the purgation of a feminized America—kicked prostrate, slapped, heel ground into "that soft breast" in order that *she* can rise, recover, "Never to forget" (23); while "the gradualist" carps, "Takes time" (22). This vengeful, violent wished-for reversal of the power relationship between black and white America, proclaimed by Amos, is an odd displacement of anger onto a feminine personification—as if America must be feminized to be conquered. "Let her lie there, panting and wild, her pain / red, running roughly through the illustrious ruin." Amos finally wishes on the feminized America the same dialogical process that African Americans have had to engage in order to survive while carrying forward their own history of being ground beneath the "great-nailed boots" of white America: "Then shall she rise, recover. / Never to forget" (23). This passage seems to parody the interracial possibility exemplified in the early years of the Student Nonviolent Coordinating Committee, which called itself "the beloved community," and briefly made a place for the exploration of interracial camaraderie, friendship, and sexuality.

"The ballad of Edie Barrow:"—a strikingly formalist moment—announces itself to the reader, its colon preceding the narrative of free indirect discourse. Edie's story of how she gives herself to a "gentile boy" to be rejected by him for one of his own kind is a "surface divergence" (Jones 200), distracting the reader from Brooks's comment on formalism and her own copious use of the ballad form in her earlier poetry. Brooks offers Edie's ballad as a counterpoint to Amos's prayer. The lyricality and alternating end rhyme disguise its cynicism. Also, Edie's metonymic lament that her situation as compromised woman will be as a "hungry tooth in my breast" (23) corresponds to Amos's vengeful prayer that "Great-nailed boots . . . heel-grind that soft breast" of America, the metaphorical woman. In the women subjects, Mrs. Sallie, Ida (Prophet Williams's dead wife), Great-great Gram, Yvonne, Mazola, Edie, and of course Pepita, Brooks shows how history is inscribed on the bodies of women. The lyric regressions in the poem are sustained by the female subjects: Yvonne, Mazola, Edie, and, as we shall see, even Pepita. "The ballad of Edie Barrow" represents more than any other passage the suppression of the lyric. Though Edie's "Gentile boy" will wed "the gentle Gentile," who "will be queen of his rest," she, Edie, "shall be queen of his summerhouse storm." In other words, Edie remains his mistress as he remains her "Gentile boy," as the lyric continues to contaminate even "the new [Black] art and anthem."

The corrupted (hetero)sexuality in the Mecca, alluded to earlier, is humorously and cynically revealed when Prophet

Williams, the other charlatan Christian, is revisited, this time as a purveyor of love potions and elixirs: "Drawing and Holding Powder," "Attraction Powder," "Black Cat Powder," "'Marvelous Potency Number Ninety-one'" (25).

Ironically, it may be that Prophet Williams, with all his elixirs for the fixing of heterosexual relationships, is engaged in a homosexual affair. We have already been told previously that he "reeks with lust for his disciple" (6) and that his wife, Ida, is dead. We are not told the gender of the disciple. Perhaps, "Enrico Jason," whom we encounter among the elixirs and potions in this late segment of the poem, is Prophet's disciple: "Enrico Jason, a glossy circular blackness / . . . soon will lie beside his prophet in bright blood, / a rhythm of stillness / above the nuances" (25).

The "bright blood," the oxymoron "a rhythm of stillness," and "nuances" might all refer to coital and postcoital acts between the two men. Brooks presents a much more sympathetic portrait of homosexual men in "Spaulding and Francois," the eighth part of her exquisite multipart poem, "A Catch of Shy Fish" (*Selected Poems* 126–127). The homosexual relationships, like most of the relationships in the Mecca, are corrupted also; homosexuality is also unacceptable within the circle of black nationalist practitioners.

As the narrator's frantic pace through the fragmented community of language-users accelerates, for the first time, she addresses the missing girl, Pepita, directly: "How many care, Pepita?" Catalogues of would-be witnesses, "hollowed, scant, played-out deformities," with odd and ordinary names, are confronted with the narrator's increasingly desperate question: "Staley and Lara . . . . Eunie . . . . Simpson . . . Bixby and June . . . these three Maries . . . . Darkara . . . Aunt Tippie, Zombie Bell, Mr. Kelly . . . Gas Cady . . . . Queenie King" (25–26). "These little care," answers the narrator. "Wezlyn, the wandering woman" and "Insane Sophie," the screaming woman, mark again the loneliness and marginality of women in the Mecca. Perhaps this mass indifference to Pepita's absence and ultimate death reflects Brooks's experience of the black proletariat's unresponsiveness to "European models," as she intimates, in *Report from Part One*, when she began to offer her first writing workshop to members of the Blackstone Rangers teen gang in 1967: "'Iambic pentameter,' they twittered. 'Hmmmm. Oh yes, iambic pentameter. Well, now.'. . . Presently I gave up imposing my exercises—and we became friends" (195).

Having found his own voice, Alfred returns and, for the first time, in a direct testimony rejects the tutelage of his white Western masters. He muses, in direct address, on the sacrifice he must make:

'A violent reverse.
We part from all we thought we knew of love
and of dismay-with-flags-on. What we know
is that there are confusion and conclusion.
Rending.
Even the hardest parting is a contribution. . . .
What shall we say?
Farewell. And Hail! Until Farewell
            again.' (27–28)

The second, fifth, and sixth lines signal the painful parting with the lyric testament—at least in the Mecca, emerging now as an actual and symbolic place of mourning. Lyric signifies sex, the feminine, racial and artistic contamination by the white West, which is the decayed edifice, the Mecca. What can be reclaimed or recuperated? Certainly not Pepita and certainly not the lyric, as the narrator takes the reader closer to the reality of the "accident."

The narrator reemerges with the startlingly sarcastic narrative of the "sixtyish sisters, the twins with floured faces," holdovers from the Talented Tenth, who are sharply juxtaposed to an equally satiric narrative of "Way-out Morgan," a bitter paramilitarist, "sinfully lean . . . fills fearsomely / on visions of

Death-to-the-Hordes-of-the-White-Men!   Death!"(28).   The
overdetermined signification alerts the reader once again to the
psychic deterioration, due to racism, festering in the Mecca (in
the Movement, and in the country). Way-out, as his name sug-
gests, has been driven to the margins of sanity (and legality) by
his encounters with violent racism in Chicago and Mississippi, as
he remembers "three local-and-legal beatings. . . . Remembering
his Sister / mob-raped in Mississippi" (28). Morgan envisions,
like Amos, a vengeful sacrifice, justified by the rhetoric of
"Blackness stern and blunt and beautiful, / organ-rich Blackness
telling a terrible story" (29). Way-out also remembers deaths of
"mates in the Mississippi River, / mates with black bodies once
majestic," and reminds us as well of the real bodies of Emmet Till
in 1955, James Chaney, Michael Schwerner, Andrew Goodman
in 1964, and countless other murdered "mates" dredged up from
the Mississippi River and other rivers in the South.

    However, Way-out, a survivor of a horrific past, is unable to
tell his own story in order to protect himself from his ghosts.
Dori Laub, Felman's co-author of *Testimony*, says of a Holocaust
survivor unable to come to terms with the horrific events of
her past what might be said of Way-out. She has structured her
whole life "as a substitution for the mourned past," leading to
an "unavoidable dead-end, in which the fight against the oblit-
eration of the story could only be at the cost of the obliteration
of the audience" (Felman 78–79). Way-out "postpones" sex with
"a yellow woman in his bed . . . to consider" his vision of
"Ruin." One might say Way-out "obliterates" his audience—or
perhaps it is Brooks who obliterates the audience. She cannot
resist playing upon the irony of a "yellow woman" in the
"organ-rich Blackness" of Way-out's bed, a story her poetry tells
time and again, beginning with "The Ballad of Chocolate Mab-
bie" in her first published adult volume of poems, *A Street in
Bronzeville*, as Mabbie awaits her "saucily bold Willie Boone,"
who wears a "lemon-hued lynx" on his arm (*Selected Poems* 7).

However, the final depiction of Alfred, "lean at the balcony leaning" posits sacrifice and offers hope, and perhaps renascence:

> And steadily
> an essential sanity, black and electric,
> builds to a reportage and redemption.
> A hot estrangement. A material collapse
> that is Construction. (31)

The narrator presents the body of the murdered Pepita, "beneath the cot" of her murderer, Jamaican Edward. Pepita's body and Jamaican Edward are the last of the more than fifty subjects the narrator shows us. Though the reader has never known Pepita, her body and her death provide that "essential sanity," the final relief, and a grounding in chaotic space. The narrator quotes to the reader Pepita's own childishly lyrical words and rhyming couplet: "'I touch'—she said once—'petals of a rose. / A silky feeling through me goes!'" (31). The reader, as Alfred in the passage above, must see construction from material collapse, must in seeking reality, as Felman suggests, "explore the injury inflicted by it" (28), must find the language ("reportage") to reemerge from the paralysis induced by it, must "move on." It is uncertain the reader can move on. The fragments of the lost or sacrificed still hold her. Perhaps Brooks is making the reader attend to "In the Mecca" as a wake, a wake for her earlier work, rich with lyric testimony. Perhaps the death of Pepita is an unwitting trope for black women's loss of status in the black movement as the urgency of Black Power begins to shape relations between black men and black women as advocates of black liberation.

Ultimately, "Mecca," with all of its historical, metaphorical, cultural, political weight for black Americans, is a place/space of dissolution and desolation—a dystopic space. The modes of narration remain split, which signifies the impossibility of reconciliation inside the Mecca. There is a possibility of a new birth of language—outside the Mecca—the possibility of something "black and electric" rising out of the rubble, perhaps even out of the dead Pepita's "chopped chirpings oddly rising" (28). Perhaps the lyric will haunt African American poetry as the slave narrative haunts white American literature.

I have used "In the Mecca" as a stratagem to signal the space of women poets within and without the new cultural space of B/blackness. Brooks confronts the complexity of the work black nationalism must do for the so-called "nation" to transform black people in America, and indeed the work poetry must do. Both black nationalism and poetry must come to terms with death and killing—of dreams, of psyches, of relationships, of material sustenance, of potential, of optimism, of people. "Can they?"—the poem seems to ask. Brooks sets this challenge for herself as poet and nascent nationalist, beginning to take her place within the circle of the Black Arts Movement.

I am constructing the moment of the publication of "In the Mecca" as the opening for black women poets to articulate their own cultural imperatives. Brooks's act of removing her work from a major publishing house to an independent press— at a time when the work of black women writers was becoming a publishing commodity—was a radical act because of which she assumed within the Black Arts Movement the status of elder at the age of fifty-one. Her simultaneous rejection of perceived white cultural control and her embracing of the new black expressivity opens space for the varied voices of black women poets beginning to publish in greater numbers than during the New Negro Renaissance, nearly fifty years before. Brooks explores the possibility of new space, new speech, and new agency in "After Mecca," the second part of *In The Mecca*, which I discuss in chapter 3. I construct its male-focused space of occasional, hortatory, eulogistic poems as the ground upon which black women poets must contend for voice.

CHAPTER 3

Queen Sistuh

BLACK WOMEN POETS AND THE CIRCLE(S) OF BLACKNESS

> I did not, when a slave, understand the deep
> meanings of those rude, and apparently inco-
> herent songs. I was myself *within the circle*,
> so that I neither saw nor heard as those with-
> out might see and hear. . . .
>
> —*Narrative of the Life of Frederick Douglass*,
> Frederick Douglass

As BLACK POWER Movement practitioners appealed to black American people to turn away from white systems of power and cooption, its "theoretical twin," the Black Arts Movement, mandated a similar move away from Western and European modernist cultural models. And both Black Power and Black Arts movements demanded that blacks in the funky United States turn to the practice of an historic, contemporary, and unitary African American culture. As I discussed in chapter 2, the loss of lyric space and the loss of the lyric's place in African American poetry caused openings of other spaces of mourning, as black Americans gave up their reliance on various Euro-American discourses of freedom and rights: The Declaration of Independence, The Constitution of the United States, The Bill of Rights, *Brown vs. the Board of Education of Topeka, Kansas,* The 1964 Civil Rights Bill, The Voting Rights Act of

1965, to name a very few. The practice of black American culture is as old as the presence of Africans in the putative New World. The Black Power and the Black Arts movements impelled black Americans to relearn it, or, in some cases to learn it for the first time. Many black people in the United States of the so-called baby-boomer generation, like myself, knew nothing about any activism that predated the Montgomery Bus Boycott (1955) and the integration of Central High School in Little Rock, Arkansas (1957). I had some sense from my family members who passed on post-Reconstruction stories of Juneteenth, post–World War I stories of memorizing poems by Paul Laurence Dunbar in celebration of Negro History Week, and assertions of pride about other black firsts and worthies—for example, Percy Julien, Charles Drew, Alain Locke, George Washington Carver, and Langston Hughes.

For the sake of this discussion, I wish to imagine black American culture to be a system of circles constantly being redrawn and reshaped along race, gender, sex, class, and community lines—sometimes concentric and constricting, sometimes overlapping and inclusive, and sometimes spiraling out of bounds. As we neophytes of the new "Blackness" paced the boundaries "without the circle," longing to participate, we felt our situation a reversal of that which Douglass meditates upon in this chapter's epigraph. For Douglass, in this passage, being "without the circle," achieving distance, produced knowledge of the "deep meanings" of the slave songs and also knowledge of a history—in Africa—prior to slavery.[1] For us, prospective practitioners of the "new" blackness, being "without the circle" produced anxiety and crises of identity. We, perhaps, feared we lacked the authenticity of experience from which Douglass, former slave and eternal freedom fighter, spoke. Black Arts Movement cultural workers sought reimmersion in the source of "those crude, and apparently incoherent songs." But being within was not without its sacrifices. The boundary of that "in-

nermost circle" of blackness was heavily policed by the "new
black nationalist patriarchy."

In an early clever poem, Don L. Lee asserts that the "black-
woman's" femininity is a reflection of her man's masculinity":

> blackwoman:
> is an
> in and out
> rightsideup
> action-image
> of her man . . . .
> in other
> (blacker) words;
> she's together
> if
> he
> bes
> (Brooks, ed. 102)

"Woman" is elided with "Black." No space for black women's
multiple identities is given between race and gender in the best
of all possible Black (male) worlds. And there is no space for
black women to be identified as nonconcentric to or separate
from black men. Though her sense of who she is may depend
upon her man's state of readiness, according to the speaker in
the Lee poem, "blackwoman" must be capable of *acting*—like a
man.

HOW BLACK WOMEN POETS configured themselves in relation to
the Black Arts Movement—from within, at the margins, and
"without the circle"—is the main concern of chapter 3. What
themes do these poets allow themselves to address? And how are
these themes received by black men "within the circle"? How do
black women poets theorize their relations "within" and "with-
out" the circle? Do black women poets create a counter-black

counter-public? How do they mediate the masculine-centered poetics and gender politics?

In his 1968 article, "Toward a Black Aesthetic," which discussed the role of the black critic, Hoyt W. Fuller has no hesitancy in calling for the *"reclamation and indoctrination of black art and culture"* (Mitchell, ed. 204, emphasis added). And, as Henry Louis Gates, Jr., reflected in the late 1980s, neither students, writers, critics, nor people in the street were "immune" to this "infectious movement of letters," which created "a broad community of black readers, from the streets of Harlem to the hallowed halls of Harvard" (*Figures in Black* xxv). This "Black Aesthetic moment" led, as well, to the publishing of new works and the reprinting of past works, that is, repetition, of the "Afro-American tradition" (xxvii).

The Black Arts Movement's sources are, in fact, multiple and so are its protagonists and detractors. Amiri Baraka (*Eulogies* 96) claims that James Baldwin's 1964 play, *Blues for Mister Charlie*, "announced" the Black Arts Movement because of its uncompromising attack on the murderous systems of white racism and its affirmation of black resistance. (Strikingly, Baraka did not make this claim until Baldwin's funeral in 1987.) Critics as disparate as the black nationalist Larry Neal and the poststructuralist Henry Louis Gates, Jr.,[2] assert that Baraka's establishment of the Black Arts Repertory Theater in New York in 1964 gave birth to this powerful new era of black expressivity in which both women and men participated and actively established that black art/culture was symmetrical with politics in its importance to black liberation. Baldwin's influence on the Black Arts Movement would soon be erased, because of his homosexuality, by many of its male proponents, chiefly Eldridge Cleaver.

Every person who would call herself "black" had to *recover* the black past, *discover* her black self, and *proselytize* for a black world, as critic and arbiter Larry Neal posited:

A main tenet of Black Power is the necessity for Black people to define the world in their own terms. The Black artist has made the same point in the context of aesthetics. The two movements postulate that there are in fact and in spirit two Americas—one black, one white. The Black artist takes this to mean that his primary duty is to speak to the spiritual and cultural needs of Black people. Therefore, the main thrust of this new breed of contemporary writers to confront the contradictions arising out of the Black man's experience in the racist West. (Mitchell, ed., 184)

Also according to Neal, "all" black artists and Black Arts practitioners—if they "be Black"—are in service to "a long overdue debt to the Black man" (195). Neal requires heterosexuality of these artists and practitioners; for he quickly assigns homosexual males to "hell holes" (190) and ascribes gender dysfunction to lesbians (195). Celibacy is not possible, given the Black Arts Movement prescription of procreation, with black women quickly becoming custodians of the revolution. Despite his privileging of black men and male artists, Neal would probably allow that black arts could very likely be practiced *by* anybody black *for* anybody black.

Sacrifice is just as crucial to the practice of Black American culture "within the circle" of the Black Arts Movement as it was within the various cadres of the Black Power Movement and as it was within "the beloved community" of SNCC in its pre–Black Power days. In the case of SNCC, the sacrifice might well have meant the loss of one's life for the greater goal of racial equality within U.S. culture. In the case of the Black Power Movement, one must be prepared to die in defense of or kill for revolutionary racial justice, which would spell the end of white domination of black people, as Sonia Sanchez chants in "Life Poem:"

shall I die . . .
>   a sweet/death
>   a sweet/blk/death . . . .
>   . . . . move in to
>>   killing hood.   for
> my people.
>>   for my beautiful/
>>   blk/
>>   people.
>>   (Brooks, ed. 143)

In *New Day In Babylon,* William L. Van Deburg claims that "during the Black Power years, angry black writers evidenced their rejection of the civil rights movement's nonviolent ethic by creating characters who vigorously called for whitey's eradication. . . . Holding to this notion that it sometimes took an inhuman act to end inhumanity, Afro-American writers defended social violence as necessary to self-defense and nation-building" (283). And, as evidenced above in Sanchez's poem, Black women poets were among those "angry black writers."

Unlike the coded conventions adhered to by black women poets of the Harlem Renaissance, who embedded their racial politics in "genteel language" and the "least controversial of tropes" (Wall 14), Black Arts Movement women poets appropriated the rhetoric often attributed in the main to their male comrades and counterparts (Heacock 30), which spelled the impending dissolution of "whitey," while subscribing, through lyric expression, to the dictates of womanhood within the circle. They, like black men, would use "culture as a weapon" of construction and destruction (Van Deburg 1993, 285). However, as hardworking as they were in the production of their poetry, their work was often underrepresented or misrepresented in the journals, anthologies, and other publications of the day.[3]

Despite its nationalist/separatist gestures, the Black Arts Movement changed the reception of black culture worldwide. However, its theory of redemptive/compensatory manhood absorbed the "race" as a whole in the United States. The New World social castration collectively experienced by black people feminized the "race." Given this circumstance, the "race" must become "men" and move violently past this historic and collective emasculation, as evidenced in Nikki Giovanni's popular 1968 poem, "The True Import of the Present Dialogue, Black vs. Negro," from her first volume, *Black Feeling Black Talk*, in which "Negroes" are exhorted to throw off the shackles of whiteness and take on the mantle of blackness, as the poem moves spasmodically to its violently suggestive last stanza:

Can we learn to kill WHITE for BLACK
Learn to kill niggers
            Learn to be Black men (20)

By the final line, the reader becomes convinced the speaker wants the "we," the collectivity, the "race" to become "men"— not just "Black"—even as the blackness is emphasized, in the style of the day, with the uppercase "B." The lower-case "m" seems to signify the lesser importance of "men," but not really, for its terminal position accentuates its crucial value. The space between "Black" and "men" signals its inclusive possibilities for all members to "come on in." Perhaps the erasure of black women is intentional to project the urgency for unity and solidarity, to focus on the possibilities for sameness as opposed to identities that might distract the race from one's becoming "Black men."

In her popular (and feminist) 1968 "woman poem," Giovanni reverses the prevailing image of black women as impervious by deftly appropriating the trope of impotence, that is, "castration," reserved by black men for themselves, and extending it to women:

Its [sic] having a job
They won't let you work
Or no work at all
Castrating me
Yes, it happens to women too. (24–25)

As Toni Morrison, in *Beloved*, enters into dialogue with white and black male historians who have denied the story of black women's vitality within the community of slaves, Giovanni enters into dialogue with and corrects white and black social scientists who have refused to acknowledge how institutionalized racism and sexism have also stunted the economic viability of black women: "Yes, it happens to women too." Despite the lack of space "blackwoman" is given in Don L. Lee's poem of the same name, discussed previously, the lines she "is an / in and out / *rightsideup* / action-image / of her man" (emphasis added) seem to contradict the terminal lines, "she's together / if / he / bes," which translates "blackwoman" through "her man." More than a mere "reflection" of her man's togetherness, the poem seems to imagine that "blackwoman" is a corrected version of "her man," that is, more than a man. "In other / (blacker) words," Black Arts poems are corrective texts, deflating racist stereotypes, reframing and revising history, and creating new mythologies. We will see more of this strategy as we proceed through this chapter; and we will see how this renaming, reframing, and revising continue to be deployed by black feminists and lesbian feminists, particularly in Ntozake Shange's *for colored girls who have considered suicide/when the rainbow is enuf* in chapter 4 and in Audre Lorde's *The Black Unicorn* in chapter 5.

"After Mecca," the second part of Brooks's *In The Mecca*, deals with the aftermath of the dissolution of community represented in the first part of the collection, "In the Mecca," as discussed in chapter 2. The mourning is not over. The epitaphlike poems, "To A Winter Squirrel" and "Boy Breaking Glass," address the desolation and waste of humanity, which always concern Brooks and converge with the Black Arts Movement's emphasis on the vagaries of life for black people in America:

> A sloppy amalgamation.
> A mistake.
> A cliff.
> A hymn, a snare, and an exceeding sun. (37)

These four lines signify the history of Africans in the New World: a displacement so profound, captured at the edge of a civilization where the only refuges are endless song (that is, hope) and unending work. We proceed into increasingly masculine space with the eulogies, "Medgar Evers" and "Malcolm X," black male leaders assassinated in 1964 and 1965, respectively. Medgar Evers, field secretary for the NAACP in Mississippi, was shot and killed outside his home in Jackson, Mississippi, in 1963 by a white man, Byron de la Beckwith, convicted of that murder after more than thirty years of legal evasion and final prosecution. Malcolm X, who changed his name to El Hajj Malik El-Shabazz in 1964, was gunned down by three black men at the Audubon Ballroom in Harlem in 1965. Malcolm's rhetoric on black American oppression had shifted from a domestic to an international arena; he claimed protection under the United Nations' Declaration of Human Rights and even took the name of his newly established Organization of Afro-American Unity from that of the Organization of African Unity in East Africa. The poems appear on facing pages, yoking together the two diametrically different icons of black freedom and liberation. Each poem is dedicated to a man: "Medgar Evers" is dedicated to Charles Evers, older brother of the slain Evers, and "Malcolm X" is dedicated to Dudley Randall, founder of Broadside Press and soon to become Brooks's publisher. (Martin Luther King died only three months after the publication of *In The Mecca*.)

"Two Dedications," a sequence of two poems, a "diptych" (Melhem) places the poet almost two weeks apart at two extremely different events honoring public art. "The Chicago Picasso," a poem commissioned by Mayor Richard Daley to inaugurate the renowned modernist's steel sculpture, which he unveiled at the Civic Center in August 15, 1967, before an audience of 50,000 to Seiji Ozawa leading the Chicago Symphony. The poem critiques the distance "the Western field" puts between "man" and art. "The Wall," the second, longer poem, was written upon the occasion of the completion of the mural of Black "Heroes" (Brooks's portrait included) painted on a slum building on Chicago's South Side. Brooks reads at the latter event on August 27 and captivates with her words the black audience, ready to "yield [her] hot trust." Brooks juxtaposes and exposes the contradictions between (white) Western culture and the recovered/discovered Black culture.

The last three poems, "The Blackstone Rangers," "Sermon on the Warpland," and "The Second Sermon on the Warpland" leave us in the street, in the "wild weed." In "Blackstone Rangers," which reflects Brooks's real life experience of offering a writing workshop to members of the Blackstone Rangers—"Jeff," "Gene," "Geronimo," and "Bop"—male gang leaders, learn to "edit, fuse/unfashionable damnations and descent" into poetry of "monstrous . . . grace," while Mary Ann, a gang girl, "A Rangerette," looks on at her "laboring lover," settling for the "bleat of not-obese devotion," in the background. The two "Sermons," one opening with an epigraph attributed to notoriously influential cultural nationalist Maulana Ron Karenga and the other dedicated to Chicago activist Walter Bradford, which close the volume, exhort the imagined community ("sisters, brothers . . . brothers, sisters") to "turn the River," to prepare for "the coming hell and health together," to meet "the brash and terrible weather" with "lithe love" (49) and to "Live and go out./Define and/medicate the whirlwind" (53).

While the leadership in the whirlwind is male proletariat— "A garbage man is dignified / as any diplomat"—women, like "Big Bessie," do their work at the margins, "in the wild weed" (54)."In the wild weed she is a citizen, / and is a moment of highest quality; admirable" (54).

After the desolation of the woman-centered "In the Mecca," the poems of "After Mecca" seem to cede the public to black men. Big Bessie, more subversive than the victimized Pepita, the powerless Mrs. Sallie, the impoverished "Merdice" of "Winter Squirrel," appears in the wild weed after the male-centered text of the second part to remind those in the leadership of their responsibility to changing the lives of those who occupy the margins.

> Circles are self-completing
> where your back was
> so your face is
> Seeing blindly now
> through musical houses—lives
> will not hide you
> but make your tomorrow nation
> verbatim songs
> of your present condition. (Loftin 14)

The circle is dangerously constricting in Elouise Loftin's poem, "These Circles." Repetition is not always a productive thing, despite how its use has enabled and still enables African-American culture to survive. Sometimes repetition signals a cessation of language, proliferates tropes silencing dissent and difference, resonates with prescriptive codes; and sometimes its incantatoriness offers false consolation or a false sense of power, which results in stasis.

The establishment of institutions by, for, and about the

transmission of black culture was the business of the Black Arts Movement and was crucial to remaking the black soul and a "Negro to Black" conversion. Africa was touted as the center, and Europe and its institutions were "heel-ground" into the dirt. The black nationalist premise of self-help informed these institutions of art and politics. In the context of Carolyn Rodgers article, "Black Poetry—Where It's At," referred to in chapter 2, a combination of "teachin/rappin" and "covers-off" poetry was pressed into the service of broadcasting appropriate "African" values.

Jayne Cortez's rowdy reprimand, "Race," from her 1969 collection *Pissstained Stairs and the Monkey Man's Wares*, works overtime to prescribe appropriate sexuality for black men. The speaker assumes an odd Biblical authority and addresses malevolent taunts to a monolithic black man, emphasized by the capitalization of "Black Man" and the nonmetrical lines and close rhyme of the degrading ascription, "breeder,"—"of the great race / of black faces." From there, the narrative devolves into a twisted Abraham and Isaac diatribe, warning black men to "slaughter" their "Faggot Queer Punk Sissy" sons, "unable to grasp the fact / and responsibility / of manhood black." The "Race called Faggot" is of no use to the "race" and the bringing-on of the "revolution," which will not include "this lost tribe of whimpering sons." After enunciating every stereotype of homosexual men—from biological determinism to cross-dressing to pedophilia—in a scatological riff that becomes typical of Cortez's apocalyptic poetics, the speaker denounces black male homosexuality and challenges the undifferentiated "black man" to rid "our sons" of its scourge.

Another tactic of the conversion process was to divide the audience by articulating what blackness is not, conversely identifying who can be a member. Clearly, homosexuals, especially male homosexuals, had only counterrevolutionary currency and had to be eradicated in order to masculinize the "race." This model of reeducation, however, razed the canonical fortress and cleared the way for a multicultural generation of "guerillas," particularly feminists, gays, and lesbians in the 1980s.

Black college students at historically black and those at predominately white colleges and universities were the foot soldiers of the Black Power and Black Arts movements and played a major role in reeducating their peers and elders in the new black consciousness. They were indispensable in the conversion process inside and outside the academy. They demanded that different books be read, that Black Arts/Black Power proponents be brought to campus as speakers, that black scholars and intellectuals and activists be hired in academic departments, and moreover that black studies programs be created. Black college students were radical agents of institutional change—just as they had been in the segregated South. However, they were often targets of criticism and ridicule from those who narrowly constructed the politics of location. Tending to the life of the mind was sometimes seen as a dangerous distraction from developing the black community. If one were to be a student, then one had better be nation-building.

In her poem, "Black Students," Julia Fields (Major, ed. 49) does not differentiate among her subjects whom her speaker accuses of acts of bad faith similar to those articulated in Baraka's 1969 poem, "Poem for Halfwhite College Students." This monolithic group of black students are consumers of "Wedgewood" and "Chippendale," while "thinking Benin," the fifteenth-century West African kingdom noted for its advanced metal-working. Perceived mass ignorance of African or African-American history was a theme of much conversion poetry. And the masses were expected to submit to a counterbrainwashing in blackness.

In Sonia Sanchez's poem, "let us begin the real work (for Elijah Muhammad who has begun)," the speaker admonishes the race to reclaim black children from the social institutions of "wite/amurica" in order to "honestlee begin / nation / hood / builden"(65).

Nikki Giovanni's previously discussed "The True Import of Present Dialogue, Black vs. Negro" left audiences breathless with its harsh repetition, "Nigger / Can you kill / Can you kill". Its dozens-like resonance, its violent rhetoric and images, its castigation of white people and black people render it, like Cortez's "Race," an exemplary Black Arts Movement poem, which engages in the politics of conversion by rebuke. The challenge is for the "Nigger" (with a capital "N") to imagine a violent come-uppance against white people and to be ready to undertake it.

In his discussion of the development of black secular song, Lawrence Levine pays close attention in *Black Culture and Black Consciousness: Afro-American Folk Thought From Slavery to Freedom* to the impact of black music on the physical and psychic survival of black Americans. He conjectures on the transporting effects of the work song, which might be likened to the intent of "True Import" and "Race": "Secular work songs resembled the spirituals in that their endless rhythmic and verbal repetitions could transport the singers beyond time, make them oblivious of their immediate surroundings, and create a state of what Wilfrid Mellers has referred to as 'ritualistic hypnosis' which made it possible to persevere under the most unfavorable of circumstances" (213). "'Ritualistic hypnosis'" does not a revolution sustain. However, the Black Arts Movement proponents framed their appeals to black people's consciousness in the Afro-American tradition of the perorating, single elevated figure summoning transformation: "Those of us in the Black Arts Movement . . . wanted our poetry to *be* black music" (Baraka, *The Autobiography* 127).

Earlier I made a cursory remark about the reification by black poets of black music during the Black Arts Movement era. As far as most Black Arts Movement exponents were concerned, poetry and any other form of writing could only *hope* to approach the authenticity of the black experience represented in the music of Africans in the New World—and black women poets' poems were no less adulatory of every black musician from Duke Ellington to Ray Charles's back-up singers, the Raelets.

"The Forms of Things Unknown," Stephen Henderson's groundbreaking monograph, introduces the 1973 anthology, *Understanding the New Black Poetry*; he presents an extensive and exuberant discussion of "black music as poetic reference" (46–61). He generates ten types of black music references in black poetry and discusses how poets from (Jean) Toomer to Hughes and Brooks to Sanchez, Madhubuti/Lee, and A. B. Spellman pay homage to the music. Because of black poets' tradition of honoring black music and musicians, Henderson tries to collapse the distinction between "song" and "poem" in order to bring the poem closer to the "musical ideal": "A poem may thus differ from performance to performance just as jazz performances of 'My Favorite Things' would. Moreover, it implies that there is a Black poetic mechanism, much like the musical ones, which can transform even a Shakespearean sonnet into a jazz poem, the basic conceptual model of contemporary Black poetry. The technique, the fundamental device, would be improvisation, lying as it does at the very heart of jazz music" (61).

This obeisance to black music, of course, did not begin with the Black Arts Movement. Homage to the music has been a part of the African-American literary tradition since the nineteenth century, as demonstrated in the passage from Frederick Douglass's *Narrative of a Slave*, used as an epigraph at the beginning of this chapter. DuBois's meditation on the "sorrow songs" and the poetry of the Harlem Renaissance poets, chiefly Hughes and Sterling Brown, continued the legacy of honoring black music. However, as I demonstrate in the following poems, written during the era of the Black Arts Movement, the

homage to black music was part of the process of cultural reviv-
ification. One's black music literacy was also a measure of one's
authentic blackness, and even more prized was one's ability to
identify jazz vocalists and instrumental soloists upon hearing the
first few notes. The poem was only instrumental to gaining this
knowledge.

In "Dreams," Nikki Giovanni remembers a childhood fan-
tasy of wanting to be "a raelet," indicative of where the poet
stands in relation to the musician. Though she might have to
give up her childhood dream of being a Raelet, she will settle
for being "a sweet inspiration"—a reference to The Sweet In-
spirations who sometimes recorded on their own but are more
well-known in R&B circles for backing-up Aretha Franklin
during the seventies. In either case—Raelets or Sweet Inspira-
tions—poets are placed in the background of the main act,
back-up to the back-ups, not quite the lyric.

Although often cast as a poor relation of black music, black
poetry is a chief repository of semiotic representation of leg-
endary black singers and musicians. Refusing to accept any lit-
erary forebears—either black or white—as their models or
mentors, most Black Arts Movement poets began to construct
their own lineage of "hollers, chants, arwhoolies, and ballits"
(Jones, *Home* 106). A favorite technique of Black Arts poets was
to use language to create the sounds of the improvisational/ex-
perimental antilyrical expression of the new jazz forms; as in
Sonia Sanchez's provocative "a/coltrane/poem":

> (softly   da–dum–da da da da da da da da da da/da dum
> till it   da da da da da da da da da
> builds   da–dum- da da da
> up   da–dum. da. da. da. this is a part of my
> favorite things. (71)

Richard Rogers and Oscar Hammerstein's "My Favorite
Things," from *The Sound of Music,* the quintessential tribute to

the Great White Way, became a trope of Coltrane's revisionist and visionary project. In Sanchez's hands, it becomes an instrument of poetry to incite the imagined (Black) community against "DEAD . . . WITEWESTERN/SHIT." Earlier in the poem, Sanchez alludes to *A Love Supreme*, a later Coltrane recording exemplifying his spiritual commitment to the expression of his music, as a way for black people out of "our passsst"and into "our futureeeeee"(69). John Coltrane, who died in 1966 leaving a powerful discographic legacy, had become a cultural hero, and there was no dearth of paeans to his genius. Coltrane's impact on black cultural consciousness has been compared to Malcolm X's impact on black political consciousness. Coltrane's untimely death at age forty makes his influence on the contemporary jazz and artistic cultures all the more pervasive.

Black women singers are central figures in the pantheon/ loa of black American culture, and poems in homage to black women solo singers are legion in the tradition of Afro-American poetry. Black women poets pay their respects. In "a poem for nina simone to put some music to and blow our nigguh/ minds," Sanchez invokes the late singer/performer, Nina Simone, who publicly supported the Civil Rights Movement during the 1960s and pointedly changed her performance style and her repertoire to give voice to the new black militancy, to allow her music to influence the "nigguh / mind[s]" of the "young brothers/sisters": "to be mo than pretty and loud . . . . / to be badder than me and you . . . . / to take the past and give it some light" (60). This transformation, too, with all of its gendered boundaries, is part of the recovery process as it sheds "light" on the teachings and achievements of previous generations.

Born Eleanora Fagan in 1915, Billie Holiday is a tragic though splendid figure in the annals of modern black music and in the hands of black women poets like Sanchez. Singing professionally by the age of fifteen, Holiday changed solo singing forever by virtue of her incisive interpretive powers. A universal icon of creativity, sexuality, and self-destructiveness, Holiday died at the age of forty-four of a drug overdose after a life of prolific music production, encounters with the criminal justice system, prolonged heroin and alcohol abuse, and "missed love" with numerous player type male individuals. The blame for Holiday's tragedy is often placed squarely on the shoulders of a predatory and corrupting white power, on whose capitalist pyre she was sacrificed to sell records, concert tickets, and newspapers. (This tragic junkie/flunky image was also exploited to push the sales of her apochryophal 1956 memoir, *Lady Sings the Blues*, which she wrote "with" William Dufty.) She becomes an unacknowledged and commodified genius. In a reverent tribute to Billie Holiday, "for our lady," Sanchez's speaker addresses directly a sanctified Holiday, mourning the impact of that stifled genius on the progress of black people. For Sanchez the fate of the black artist is profoundly linked to the fate of black people. Once again, as in the poems to Coltrane and Simone, Sanchez admires Holiday for her instrumentality to the liberation of black people. Yet Holiday's instrumentality to liberation might not have been so blighted "if someone / had loved u like u / shud have been loved" (41). The poem is layered with paradox, irony, and understatement. However, oddest of all for me is, despite her astute practice of telling it "like it damn sure is," of "teachin-rappin,'" of drawing the obverse relationship between Black people's progress and white America's, Sanchez chalks up Billie Holiday's thwarted promise to the lack of the right kind of romance in her life.

Lady Day's dying is reduced to a failure on the part of "someone . . . . some black man" to love her. This rather reminds one of the previously mentioned speculation at the beginning of chapter 1, that Aretha Franklin's ability to turn "The Thrill Is Gone" "every way but loose" was given vent because she had divorced her reputedly trifling husband, Ted White. In all fairness to Sanchez, Billie Holiday might have lived her life differently had she chosen less corrupt lovers, especially the likes of John Levy and Louis Hayes. Her life might also have been different if she had not been neglected and abused as a child, if the power relationship between men and women were more equitable, if hotels were not segregated, and if black artists—or any artists—were valued in this culture. Yet, none of these rationales attributes very much agency to Holiday or her own prodigious genius and intellectual processes.

In "liberation/poem," Sanchez critiques the blues, or rather a particular perception of the blues, as "sounds of / oppression," as only responsive to "the white man's / shit," as "struggle / strangulation / of our people" (54). She invokes and then rejects Billie Holiday's singing of "Am I Blue"; it was, in fact, not a blues song but a popular song written by Grant Clarke and Harry Akst (c. 1929), which Holiday recorded in 1941 for Columbia's Vocalion/Okeh label and sang with a "laid-back angst" (Clarke, 1994 192). Informed by the blues as most jazz singers are, Holiday recorded probably two in her life, "Billie's Blues" and "Fine and Mellow," which she wrote and sang as gentle parodies of the classic blues genre. Sanchez's poem dismisses the blues, a music that has sustained black Americans for more than a century now, as "strangulation of our people." The poem seems to say that the blues must be replaced by liberation poems or that this poem intends to liberate black people from the ideology of the blues:

> no mo.
> no mo
> blue / trains running on this track
> they all been de / railed
> am I blue?
> sweet / baby / blue /
> billie.
> no. i'm blk /
> & ready. (54)

Sanchez purposefully conflates "blue," the mood of sadness, and "blues," the music form, which embellishes the punning in this poem. We come to understand that Sanchez is exploiting the notion of the blues as a reflection of black people's depression, a fatalism that prevents concerted action, and a lack of agency that inhibits self-determination. Her misrepresentations of the blues are deliberate. Placing herself in dialogue with Holiday, the speaker challenges the legendary interrogative understatement with her own new declaration of spontaneous blackness. She even invokes Bob Dylan's "Sweet Baby Blue" to sass "billie." The scattered lineation also bespeaks a rejection of the formality of the blues twelve- or sixteen-bar constriction as well as any lyric constriction. This poem is a virtuoso deployment of "black speech as poetic reference" as well!

Nikki Giovanni's "Poem for Aretha" (Brooks, ed. 61–63) is replete with long lineation, enjambment, and catalogs of homage to the then-dubbed "Queen of Soul," Aretha Franklin. Typical of Giovanni's "teachin-rappin" style, the address shifts frenetically, sometimes addressing Franklin directly and other times castigating Franklin's unempathic public. The poem opens in the middle of a sentence, as if to announce why it has been written: "cause nobody deals with aretha—a mother with four / children—having to hit the road" (61). There are no stops in this poem emphasizing the unyielding pace an artist, like Franklin, must keep to satisfy the demands of her audiences; in this case, her black audiences, whom Giovanni accuses of "killing her [Aretha]" (62). However, one might conjecture that the speaker is also speaking loud enough to Franklin's black audiences in order that her white audiences might also hear or overhear. The poem cautions black people that Aretha does not have to: "relive billie holiday's life doesn't have / to relive dinah washington's death but who will / stop the pattern" (62).

IN THE SAME vein as Sterling Brown's 1932 poem, "Ma Rainey," who "'jes' catch hold of us, somekindaway'"(62), Giovanni's

"Aretha" is "undoubtedly the one person who put everyone on / notice" (63). Passing swiftly over the public's fascination with Franklin's troubled marital relationship as so much dross, the poem tells of Franklin's effect on her audiences, her influence on other artists, the way she revised black popular music, and her political importance. Though the poem asserts that Franklin is "more important than her music—if they must be separated," once again the artist, like Billie Holiday and John Coltrane, is legitimated within the circle because of her instrumentality to the black revolution. The poem enumerates Franklin's accomplishments during the mid- to late sixties in this energetic catalogue. Franklin is a transforming agent and the poem romanticizes her as the eye of the dynamism and fury of those portentous times: "aretha was the riot was the leader if she had said 'come let's do it' / it would have been done."

Sarah Webster Fabio's "Tribute to Duke"(Henderson, ed. 243), first published in 1969, attempts to effect call-and-response by placing two columns side-by-side on the page. The left column is a narrative of Ellington's achievements as an innovator, while the right column "worries the line" with snatches of stock blues phrases as well as lyrics from some of Ellington's (and Strayhorn's) more popular compositions, like "I Got It Bad and That Ain't Good," "Take the A-Train," and "My Solitude." This poem is more ambitious than effective; nonetheless, it exemplifies the drive to reflect in the poetry the perceived experimentalism of the music. In this unqualified homage to Ellington, the poem does not seek to make him instrumental—as if any poem could—to black liberation as the previous poems on Coltrane, Holiday, and Franklin, and exalts him in his own words, "'We love you madly,'" beyond any repudiation (246).

In her original and appealing study, *The Dark End of the Street: Margins in American Vanguard Poets*, Maria Damon explores Black Beat poet Bob Kaufman's appropriation of black music as subject and subtext of his poetry. She makes a provocative observation relevant to my own discussion of the loss of lyric space in the poetry of the Black Arts Movement. What replaces the pleasure and self-reflexivity of the lyric? The preponderance of poems of homage to Black American music/musicians by almost all the Black Arts–era poets is striking. Damon suggests that Black American poets' claims of kinship with Black American music go beyond notions of artistic symmetry: "Virtually every African-American poet, essayist, and critic, from DuBois to Hughes to Baraka to Stephen Henderson to Ntozake Shange to Houston Baker, has discussed the close ties between music and the rest of Black culture. The strong kinship Black American poets feel with Black American music restores the lyric to its original status as song, words written to accompany music and dance rituals" (68). The private, ruminative autonomy of the "lyric I" (Damon) is replaced by the historicized meditation on the music and song lyrics of Afro-American culture.

Almost any Black Arts poem represented black regional, rural, urban, southern, northern vernacular speech—without apostrophes or apologies or glossaries.

> From the "black and unknown [female] bards" who created spirituals to the unknown folk blues lyricists, to the storytellers around the kitchen tables, to the "sisters" standing in front of the churches on Sunday mornings, to the hairdressers standing over shampoo bowls and hot combs, African American women have made and continue to make their voices heard in women's spaces within vernacular culture. The womanly changes on African American vernacular traditions also manifest themselves in the jump-rope, particularly double Dutch, rhymes made by girls in a manner similar to the swaggering braggadocio found in the street rhymes of boys. Both are signifying traditions carried forward into today's hip-hop lyrics on rap recordings by both female and male artists. (Brown 103)

Black speech was used to authenticate the lesson of the poem, which, most often advanced black nationalist teachings.

Carolyn Rodgers's 1969 autobiographical poem, "Jesus Was Crucified Or: It Must Be Deep (an epic pome)," is a reading of black women's humor, a representation of black vernacular speech, and a mock epic, which plays on some of the religious caricatures in Brooks's "In the Mecca." The poem is the stage for an intergenerational confrontation on the telephone between a black mother and her ailing black revolutionary daughter, who is "runnin round wid Negroes/WHO CURSE IN PUBLIC!!!" (Stetson, ed. 181). The narrator's mother could be "St. Julia Jones," and the narrator-daughter might double as a female "Way Out Morgan." The poem is dense, moves rapidly in the typical the Black Arts Movement lowercase, interspersed with uppercase pronouncements from the mother and parenthetic asides from the daughter, and random punctuation. Rodgers is very skillful in reproducing the sound of black speech and writes to approximate the mother's through the daughter's irreverent narration of the dialogue. The poem also represents, as does Brooks's "Young Africans," spoken of earlier, the intergenerational squabbles ensuing within black communities everywhere over the new blackness.

The mother, who is a righteous Christian, expresses her chagrin with the daughter's loss of faith and professed hatred of white people, and the daughter rebounds with impudent forays into the mother's Christian propriety to which the mother is either impervious or oblivious:

(and I sd)
I don't believe—(and she sd) U DON'T BELIEVE IN
      GOD NO MO DO U?????
u wudn't raised that way! U gon die and go tuh HELL
and I sd I hoped it wudn't be NO HUNKIES there
and she sd
what do u mean, there is some good white people and
some bad ones, just like there is negroes

The put-downs escape the mother who continues on with her line of argument with a parable comparing the rude treatment

received by "uh colored woman" from a black sales clerk and
then her own polite treatment from a white bank teller: "ne-
groes don't treat / nobody right / . . . . this white man helped me
fast and nice" (182).

This cleverly recounted repartée continues with the mother
still unconvinced of the daughter's rejection of Christianity and
recommending that she read the Bible, particularly Revelations,
which the mother sees as particularly relevant to the then-con-
temporary scene: "and she sd what was in the Bible was / happ-
nin now, fire & all." The mother cautions the daughter that
"deep deep down / in yo heart u know it's true," to which the
daughter replies with the usual irreverent aside, "(and I sd) / it
must be deeeep," cleverly unpacking the meaning of her title.
The daughter bids a mocking goodbye to the mother with final
gibes at the mother's religiosity. "It must be deep" is a black ver-
nacular expression of incomprehensibility over others' refusal to
see glaring contradictions.

Women poets of the Black Arts Movement were invested in
and committed to deploying the range of Afro-American ver-
nacular speech in their assertions of "the truth" to black people.
Just as they accepted the primacy of black music, they, too, ac-
cepted the linguistic currency of quotidian black talk, which
some call "the language of the streets" (Henderson 32). How-
ever, older black women poets—like Gwendolyn Brooks,
Margaret Walker, Julia Fields, Margaret Danner, Naomi Long
Madgett—always mediated the vernacular with standard En-
glish. For the Black Arts women, black vernacular speech was
the always already, essential signifier of a black poem.

New poets—like Sanchez, Giovanni, and Rodgers, who
claimed space within the circle—were very concerned with do-
mestic and international systems of oppression. They manipu-
lated the vernacular to articulate those concerns as well as all
the tropes of revolution and liberation, including "obscenities"
and urgings and threats of violence. Madgett, Danner, and

Brooks, for example, were concerned that the work of past black writers—men and women—not be erased in the new Blackness. Danner's poem "The Rhetoric of Langston Hughes" admonishes the new black aestheticians that while they "'rap' . . . who was Blackest first" that the practice of black American culture predates their own, that Langston Hughes (1901–1967), for instance, had toiled, "for so long," in the vineyard of "so very Black A Power" (Stetson, ed. 133).

They utilized their positions as elders to speak from their own experiences of being black, to critique pretentious black nationalism, and to interpret the new consciousness, as Naomi Long Madgett claims in "Nomen" that she acknowledges her African past by keeping "the name my father gave me" and, thus, refusing to be "robbed a second time" (Stetson, ed. 129).

The Black Arts Movement marked the first time black women poets opened a public discourse on sexuality. The rejection of Western values—as if all Western values are white—also included reversing the middle-class Victorian morés of premarital propriety and the relegation of sex to a private, unnameable sphere. This, of course, coincided with the feminist challenge to women to liberate themselves and their repressed sexuality. Proud that the public should know they were sexually liberated and active, the women poets make the Black Arts Movement the stage for a foray into a liberated black women's sexuality. Though black women, like black men, are frequently represented in popular culture as sexually aggressive, the new Blackness demanded sexual submissiveness from women. In Giovanni's "Seduction" (*Black Feeling, Black Talk, Black Judgment*), the speaker announces a step-by-step process to her correct revolutionary brother of how she will seduce him. All the while, she imagines him more intent upon making the revolution than attentive to her "taking your dashiki off. . . . licking your arm . . . . and unbuckling your pants" (38). Cleverly, Giovanni inserts herself into the poem, thereby performing her

own identity in the moment as a (heterosexual) sexual being
and asserting power over the poem's object of desire, who ques-
tions the revolutionary appropriateness of the seduction:
"Nikki, / isn't this counterrevolutionary?" And why would sex
between a black man and a black woman at this moment be
"counter-revolutionary"? Because "Nikki" is taking birth con-
trol pills (that is, not making a baby, wasting seed, being pro-
miscuous) or because one or the other is married or in a
committed relationship? Or is it that "Nikki" has taken the ini-
tiative to plan the encounter? In its explicit representation of
the latter, the poem is unprecedented in African American po-
etry by women.

In returning momentarily to the theoretical kinship of
black poetry and black music, Jayne Cortez is perhaps one of
the most artful poets of what Henderson defines as "forcing the
reader to incorporate into the structure of the poem [her]
memory of a specific song or passage of a song, or even of a
specific delivery technique." Thus, her exclusion from the an-
thology, *Understanding the New Black Poetry*, is curious. Cortez
considers poetry and jazz as complementary, if not symmetrical,
in their ability to transmit black culture and consciousness. She
considers sexuality and poetry complementary, and, needless to
say, music and sexuality. Having spent much of her artistic life
with musicians, visual artists, and writers, practicing and teach-
ing the Black Aesthetic, Cortez has a very strong sense of po-
etry's mutability and permeability. In "3 Day New York Blues"
(*Scarifications*) she revises the popular "Stormy Monday Blues,"
written and composed in 1942 by Earl "Fatha" Hines, Billy
Eckstine, and Bob Crowder and, since then, sung by every male
vocalist from Mr. B., himself, to the British group Jethro Tull.
"Stormy Monday Blues" recounts its speaker's quotidian routine
according to the days of the week, beginning with going out to
work on stormy Monday, ending with kneeling down to pray
on Sunday. It was always a heavy favorite because of its black

everyman speaker. Cortez's blues is a humorous poem of sexual longing that is a compendium of stock blues phrases and images. Blues is the missing and anticipation of "my frisky whiskey money bag / cuttin mood" (15) and a "deep sea divin good feelin papa / hoppin skippin jumpin flyin / back home to me."

Tuesday through Thursday, the "groanin / moanin sanctified dignified sweetsmellin / hoochicoo" is on ice in "ole possum face new york city" until Friday. This poem, a bit raunchier than Black Arts Movement proponents could stand from a woman poet, might find itself at the margins of the circle, for its explicitness and its facility with bold expressions of female sexual desire, for example, "sweetsmellin / hoochicoo"—also unprecedented in Afro-American poetry by women.

The black woman identity reification poems were legion during this time, for example Mari Evans poem "I Am A Black Woman," first appearing on the cover of *Negro Digest*'s (later to be renamed *Black World*) annual poetry issue, in 1969, the poem was then collected in her 1970 major press volume, *I Am A Black Woman*, Nikki Giovanni's "ego-tripping," from her 1970 Broadside collection *re-creation*, Sonia Sanchez's "for blk/wooomen: the only queens of this universe" from her 1970 Broadside collection *We A BaddDDD People* constructed an archetype and venerated the Black Arts Movement's standards of black womanhood—in all their atavism and hyperbole. The subjects are found longing for historical place as they watch their mates "leap screaming to the sea" (Evans 11), or "drinking nectar with allah" (Giovanni 37), or causing the world to be "shaken" and "reborn" (Sanchez 6). The identity expressed in each poem is stabilized by each poem's catalogue of generative feats the speaker attributes to herself as a black woman. Regeneration is as key a power in the poetry of black women as strength or fierceness during this time of political and artistic/cultural revolution.

SANCHEZ'S REFLECTIVE "SISTUH," pondering her vulnerability in "a
/ needed / poem for my salvation" (40), to check oneself out,
to be more serious about the self's survival in the face of "lovers
of slick / blk / rappin" departs from the superwoman identity
poems, as does Giovanni's "Nikki Rosa," discussed in chapter 1.
Implicit in Giovanni's speaker's romanticized assertion, "I really
hope no white person ever has cause to write about me because
they never understand Black love is Black wealth" (*Black Judgment*
10), is the wish that black people take control of their stories like
Sanchez's "sistuh," who aspires to "git a phd in soniasanchezism."
To do so—that is, to discover one's black self—is to discover the
race. Self-knowledge is a paramount theme in the poetry of Black
Arts women.

"Sunni's Unveiling," a splendid poem by Elouise Loftin and
an amazing assertion of the black female body—its texture,
marks, moles, its blood and sweat, its orifices, its sensuality. She
warns her listeners of her duplicity:

> a mouth full of smiles and daggers
> and the discrimination of virgo
> here in the moon of me
> where i rise . . . . (12)

The name "Sunni" is a play on the Muslim influences tak-
ing more visible shape in black American culture, as in the ma-
jority Muslim sect, "Sunni." Loftin also plays on the diminutive
"Sonny" in African-American culture, usually reserved for boys
named after their fathers, or the female "Sunny" of the Cole
Porter ballad, "When Sunny Gets Blue," sung by many an
African American singer. Who is Sunni unveiling for? The poem
has no full stop until its final line, though the initial capitaliza-
tions of words which appear at intervals intensify the quiet hy-
perbole. "More than sweat and blood" and "More than hot-eyed
angry words," this black woman is self-defined. She is unapolo-
getic about her powers and whimsies:

I dance
Snap my fingers
at the table of my desires
Talk with the god of creation
in my mouth
Seduce life
Chew my nails and Do it
from the elbow to wrist I know the moisture of my
      nose
before tissues
I'm a Black woman
I throw my head back and laugh
at the cry of over-crowded
Knowing the smell of lies
as the whole world
sits in my belly.

Sunni's assertion of knowing "the moisture of my nose / before tissues" is an almost gratuitous expression of independence, that is, she can take care of her body's needs and desires. With the contracted statement of negritude, "I'm a Black woman," the revelation of the black and female identities occurs casually and anticlimactically at the thirty-first line of this thirty-six-line disquisition, in keeping with the notion of "unveiling." Sunni's language is confident and ironic, different from the formality of Evans's statement discussed above or Sanchez's more melismatic sounding of "i am a blk/wooOOOMAN," seeming to emphasize women's masculine derivativeness, in this dedicatory poem "for blk wooomen: the only queens of this universe" (5). The essentialized regenerative image of black women, in the last two lines of Loftin's poem may even be a bit mocking.

Black revolutionary intergenerational responsibility is interrogated by Sonia Sanchez in "blk/rhetoric"—and not uncritically: "like. *man.* / who's gonna give our young / blk / people new heroes" (15, emphasis added). Phillip Bryan Harper in his critical work, *Are We Not Men* (1995), constructs this Sanchez poem as a response to Baraka's short poem, "SOS," in which the speaker calls "all black people" who are ready for the revolution to "come on in" (Harris, ed. 218). Harper posits that Sanchez poses the question to Baraka, "Who's gonna give our young / blk / people new heroes," once they do "come on in." Sanchez theorizes a one-to-one relationship between words and deeds. Sanchez's poem voices a much-enunciated theme of the Black Arts poetry of women poets—that is, the importance of teaching and bringing others into the fold, also voiced in Brooks's "Young Africans." Sanchez's invocation of masculine energy seems to place the burden of teaching on "man." Again we see the concern for constructive behavior, as the speaker catalogues behaviors in which young black people should not be engaging: "wite / whores," "drugs," "new dances," eating "chitterlings," drinking "a 35 cents bottle of wine," "quick / fucks in the hall / way / of wite / america's mind" (16). However, couched/coded in what seem to be admonitions to young black people is a critique of behavior often attributed to black men, that is, "wite / whores." Ending on a rather petulant note, the speaker claims to be sending a distress signal for "some / one" to make the "race" live up to its promise.

In a 1970 speech to the Congress of African Peoples, Amiri Baraka warns that there is no such thing as an "instant revolution" (Van Deburg, ed. 147). However, during this time of "fire in the loins and hot rhythms" (Baraka, *Negro Digest* 6), hot rhetoric and hot heroes, venerations of black communities and frantic institution-building, and "interactive forums dedicated to the creation and celebration of communal experiences" (Van Deburg 279), black audiences easily succumbed to the illusion of the revolution's immediacy and their own invincibility. Especially "when 'armed' with their own powerful culture, black folk had little to fear from whitey" (285).

On a similar note, Sanchez examines the contradictions of the so-called "revo/lushun," again by critiquing sham and self-destructive behaviors in "So This Is Our Revolution": "nigguhs with naturals / still smoken pot drinken / shooten needles into they arms." Sanchez's speaker categorizes the behavior of "nigguhs" as the problem, as the stuff of contradictions, as the root of promiscuity—social as well as sexual. And her "nigguhs" include women:

> sistuhs fucken other sistuh's
> husbands
> > cuz the rev o lu shun dun
> freed them to fight the
> enemy (they sistuhs)
> > > yeh. (63)

Is Sanchez referring here only to the black revolution? She seems also to be referring to the impact of the concurrent sexual revolution on relationships between black women and black men and the greater sexual freedom women had begun to enjoy because of the availability of contraception. Perhaps the conflation of revolutions functions as a critique of the ways sisterhood among black women had been compromised by the bad behavior of the brothers.

In Black Arts poetry, the revolution and black people are never contemporaneous; as in the following line from Sanchez's "so this is our revolution," the revolution is in the present and black people are retrograde: "the revolushun is here / and we still / where our fathas / muthas were / twenty yrs ago." More like a teacher than a preacher, Sanchez's speaker schools the "brothas" and "sistuhs" on the lesson of self-love—a recurrent theme in the poems of this period. She cautions them to consider the necessity of public duty over private (read "sexual") desire.

> how bout a fo /
> real /revolu / shun
> with a fo / real
> battle to be fought
> outside of bed /
> room/minds.

Is there a battle being fought *inside* "of bed / room minds"? Gender inequity among (black) men and (black) women? The serious work of social change? And who is gonna be there in the morning? After the obligatory taunt at white people, "moon / people," the speaker makes clear that the problems are addressed finally to both men and women, as do most black women poets: "cmon brothas. sistuhs. / how bout a fo / / real / revolu/shun" (63).

The black and white, the black and red, the red, black, and green covers of books by African-American poets became trenchant symbols of the Black Arts Movement and filled the stacks of university libraries and the shelves of black and other independent bookstores. *Riot*, Gwendolyn Brooks's first book published by Dudley Randall's Broadside Press in the waning years of the Black Arts Movement, shows a solid black cover with a white, rough-edged spotlight—like a target or police light—off-center to the right with the word "riot" inscribed in large-point type in red ink and upper-case skewed letters. This cover and the many like it signaled new crises in the everyday world of black Americans, of which the urban riots were grave symptoms. Inside, the frontispiece bears the dedication, "For Dudley Randall, a giant in our time." Brooks, as ever, is responsive to the present—the volatile, volcanic 1960s with urban riots throughout its latter half. This "poem in three parts," *Riot*, also reflects Brooks's own artistic turbulence as a poet remaking her poetics and her politics.

"Riot," the title poem, opens with a ritualized image of the

white, patrician "John Cabot," about to be caught in a danger-
ous situation. The poem is introduced by the epigraph, "A riot
is the language of the unheard," a statement made by Martin
Luther King, who had been dead one year by the time of publi-
cation of this book in 1969. Characteristically Brooks is preoc-
cupied with the stark differences between rich and poor and
how that status is racialized, as in the previously discussed
poems which begin the second half of *In The Mecca*. Brooks
makes those differences even starker in her presentation of John
Cabot and "the Negroes." The tone and language of the poem
are bantering, parodic, alliterative, forestalling the ultimate terror
and blurring our own complicity in the narrator's presentations
of race and class differences:

> Because the Negroes were coming
> down the street.
> Because the Poor were sweaty and
> unpretty
> (not like Two Dainty Negroes in
> Winnetka)
> and they were coming toward him in
> rough ranks. . . .
> They were black and loud.
> And not detainable. And not discreet. (9)

And John Cabot goes "down in the smoke and fire / and bro-
ken glass and blood"(10); a twisted martyr with these last racist
words: "'Lord! / Forgive these nigguhs that know not what /
they do." Like the "Negroes" coming down the street in "rough
ranks," the Black Arts poets who were shouting down the white
aesthetic could be equally as rough.

"The Third Sermon" defies the epigrammatic imperative of
"The Second Sermon on the Warpland"—"This is the urgency:
Live! / and have your blooming in the noise of the Whirlwind"
(51). The large amounts of white space in the text of "Third

Sermon" render it like scatter shot as we are taken to various
scenes of crisis in the wake of the riot. There is no blooming
here. No "Big Bessie," citizen of the "wild weed," but rather:

> A woman is dead.
> Motherwoman.
> She lies among the boxes
> (that held the haughty hats, the Polish sausages)
> in newish, thorough, firm virginity—
> as rich as fudge is if you've had five pieces. (16)

The faith exemplified in Alfred's vision of "A material col-
lapse / that is Construction" in "In the Mecca" seems lost in the
strange rubble of poems in *Riot*. Carolyn M. Rodgers, an ex-
tremely versatile poet, particularly in her use of vernacular
speech and image, presents a slightly different perspective on the
"revolution" in her poem "U Name This One"—the title a
challenge to the semanticists/rhetoricians who so cavalierly de-
fine the terms of "the revolution." The speaker claims to be
ready for "uh revolution," having grown up on the streets of
"chi-town" where "uh state of peace is not known to me / any-
way." She catalogs the physical and emotional violence one as-
sociates with the urban black experience and asserts that "uh
revolution" could be no worse. As stated previously, valorization
of revolution and armed struggle was common among both
men and women poets. It seems ironic that they did not con-
sider the cultural revolution their words were engendering and
fomenting a legitimate revolution. As close as the bloody revo-
lution seemed, the machine of political repression was always
more imminent; it encroached upon the public space created
for radical challenges to the racist status quo.

THEORIZING AT THE MARGINS

From her collection *Scarifications*, "Back Home in Benin
City" (1973) by Jayne Cortez is atypical of many Black Arts

Movement paeans to mother Africa. An idealized Africa, not
unlike that which emerged during the New Negro Renais-
sance, haunted the poetry of Black Arts Movement practi-
tioners. Africa is "revolution," "lover," "progeny" as well as
"homeland," "mother/nation," and "ancestry." The specificity of
its naming and the specificity of its images of Benin—real,
imagined, physical fact, psychic state—is lush with history for
Africans. Cortez writes about Africa with an intimacy unchar-
acteristic of most Afro-American poetry.

> i am arriving at the fork of my blues
> standing on ramps of torn mouths
> sometimes confused
> sometimes free
> the heat of my soul at the entrance
> of my mistreated heart
> bound and gagged between torsos of studded knives
> stroking sperm compositions
> . . . .
> the homeland poised between lungs
> tense in the memory of fever
> hot in the chest of a returnee

Cortez alludes to, pays homage to, signifies on so much in
the cultures of diasporic Africans in this twenty-two line elegiac
tour de force. "Back Home in Benin City" reverses the trans-
Atlantic journey. She revises *Cahier d'un Retour Mon Pays Natal*
the multipart experimental poem of her Francophone literary
mentor, Aimé Cesaire.[4] (One could even say she revises Yeats's
"Sailing to Byzantium.") The "returnee" enunciates her bifur-
cated identity ("at the fork of my blues") and her liminality
("bound and gagged between torsos"). The next line, "stroking
sperm compositions" makes the male—not the female—body a
site of regeneration. Only the first word, "Here," a reference to
Benin, Africa, "the homeland," a holy and profane place, almost

unspeakable, is upper-cased. The poem is lent an experimental edge with its lower-case characters. The absence of punctuation marks distracts us from the poem's lyricism, as we wonder whether to pause or go at varying line breaks. The enjambment signifies the infinitude of Africa. Africa is the always-already.

Lucille Clifton, a Baltimorean with roots in upstate New York, plays at the margins of the circle by paying homage to poor black women's lives—the reversals and destructions. Clifton's "miss rosie," like Brooks's "Big Bessie," is not the typical icon of black womanhood embraced by the devotées of black nationalism in the Movement. Clifton's heroine is not moving in "blk / queenly / ways," as in Sonia Sanchez's poem, "black/woooooomen chant," (6). "Miss rosie" is old in a time when youth is privileged, crazy in a time when "an essential sanity" is being called for, and alone in a time when everybody is claiming a community. The speaker reminds us that miss rosie "used to be the best looking gal in georgia / used to be called the Georgia Rose" (19). Verses of history are implicit in those two lines, and we might imagine what "miss rosie" experienced migrating from Georgia to the North. "Wrapped up like garbage," "miss rosie" is not the black nationalist image of black women. The three repetitions of the phrase, "when i watch you" propel the poem forward as if the watching were a kind of homage to her debilitation, while the lower-case "i" at once accentuates the speaker's care not to be intrusive:

> i stand up
> thru your destruction
> i stand up (19)

THEORIZING "'WITHOUT'"
THE CIRCLE

In 1969, Nikki Giovanni, one of the most popular of the Black Arts Movement poets, critiqued the growing orthodoxy within the Movement in her heretical piece, "Black Poems, Poseurs and Power," which was included in her 1971 book of essays, *Gemini*. Giovanni goes for the jugulars of Ron Karenga and LeRoi Jones (not yet Baraka) and the so-called United Brothers in Newark City Council elections of 1968. Accusing them of being failed revolutionaries, Giovanni also criticizes their interpersonal blunders, false unity, and bullying tactics against dissenters. Questioning why Jones and Karenga missed the opportunity for a "massive involvement [of black people] in Black Power" in Newark, she answers her own perilous question: "Militarism, for one thing. To enter the main headquarters of the United Brothers one had to sign. This turned most people off. Then you were asked quite tersely, 'What do you want?' And if you couldn't answer concisely and accurately you were dismissed" (107).

Never one to be taken lightly, Giovanni goes on to signify on those within the circle for their orthodoxy and elitism: "If we enter electoral politics we should follow the simple formula that every Black person is a potential vote and must be welcomed and treated as such, with or without dashiki, with or without natural" (108).

A point well-taken, and better to be pragmatic than dogmatic. She notes that not only is the United Brothers not united, but its exclusionary behavior is causing division between itself and the rest of the Newark Black community. Though those who come under the harshest criticism are men, their behavior is not examined as a function/dysfunction of a predominantly male and orthodox leadership, to whom women are invisible as well as anyone else who does not display cultural nationalist trappings and politics. However, Giovanni's anger causes her focus to blur, and her argument collapses into conspiracy theorizing and an attack on James Forman for living with a white woman and their two children and still being in control of "and directing SNCC,"[5] while Stokely (Carmichael), "married to a Black woman was kicked out" (111). Strikingly, also, Giovanni compares the plight of black women within the circle of black masculinist politics to that of Jews among Gentiles. Never one to suffer black fools gladly, Giovanni directs her final barbs at black (male) artists for their insufficient understanding of the juggernaut of racism and an overestimation of the power of black culture and male generativeness.

The visibility gains of the Women's Liberation Movement were not lost on black women writers within the circle of the Black Arts Movement as they began to distance themselves from its dictates. Though they openly claimed to share an equitable power relationship with black men, black women—activists, academics, and artists alike—began to identify with feminists on issues of hierarchy, division of labor, role proscriptions, and recognition for the work they were doing "within the circle" and in the Movement(s).

The Black Woman: An Anthology was the first collection of writings by African-American women writers to problematize sexism in the context of black women's lives. Edited by the redoubtable cultural worker, Toni Cade (Bambara), and published by New American Library in 1970, most of its articles, poems, and stories championed the resourcefulness of black women and challenged the so-called necessity of black male leadership over and of black women. Articles and manifestoes like Bambara's "The Pill: Genocide or Liberation?" and "On the Issue of Roles," Frances Beale's "Double Jeopardy: To Be Black and Female," Kay Lindsey's "The Black Woman as Woman," Jean Carey Bond's "Is the Black Male Castrated?" rendered *The Black Woman* a crucial text for black feminists of the 1970s and later decades. Also included were essays, papers from study groups, and other prose pieces by black women from the civil rights, labor, socialist, and revolutionary movements of the day. Editor Cade bursts the gendered boundaries of the circle with the following radical notion: "Perhaps we need to let go of all notions of manhood and femininity and concentrate on Blackhood. . . . It perhaps takes less heart to pick up the gun than to face the task of creating a new identity, a self, perhaps an androgynous self, via commitment to the struggle"(103). (If you ask me, black political people in America can still benefit from this advice.)

After the "Preface" by Bambara, the collection formally opens with poems by three authors: Giovanni's "Woman Poem" and "Nikki Rosa," which were published originally by Broadside Press in 1969; Kay Lindsey's "Poem" and Audre Lorde's "Naturally" and "What About the Children," all of which were previously unpublished. Lindsey's hard hitting "Poem" announces itself plainly and directly. This fifteen line antilyric lyric with alternating three-line, two-line stanzas rejects maternal and sexual objectification in the first terse stanza and states the speaker's belief that "valor" for a woman need not "take place inside her" (17).

The speaker refuses the black nationalist privileging of motherhood as the primary role for women, the manner in which motherhood is naturalized, black women's instrumentality, and the vaunted revolution. The final two lines of "Poem" draw a comparison between racism and sexism, by using segregation in public accommodations as an analogy to the status of black women. The use of anger as a vehicle for critique often leads to faulty analysis, as was demonstrated in the Giovanni piece, "Black Poems, Poseurs and Power." Lindsey becomes overzealous in her efforts to expose the contradictions of male chauvinism in the black movement by conflating a signpost of segregation, "sitting in the back of the bus," with King's strategies of civil disobedience or passive resistance. Does she perhaps mean that the customary acceptance of second-class citizenship—as black person and as a woman—is as old-hat as Martin Luther King's leadership. Were King and nonviolent resistance only fads? Segregation was outlawed over the bodies of thousands of people, including King's. Like Giovanni's nod to black

nationalism in her attack on relationships between black men
and white women in the "Black Poems, Poseurs" above, Lindsey
gestures toward black nationalism by rejecting nonviolence. But
she construes nonviolence as the acceptance of second-class sta-
tus. Lindsey's poem is indicative of the ambivalence black
women were feeling about leaving the circle.

Three years later, Audre Lorde's "Who Said It Was Simple,"
From a Land Where Other People Live (1973), casts its gauntlet
down next to Lindsey's. She theorizes on the complexities of
privilege and oppression. Framing the narrative is the caution-
ary proposition on the dangers of repressed anger, which she
compares to a tree with main roots shattering its branches be-
fore they bear fruit (39).

From the "almost white counterman" who passes a "wait-
ing brother" to serve a group of white women first to those
same "ladies," who are oblivious to the "slavery" of their race
privilege, Lorde provides a lesson on her opening "tree of
anger" aphorism. The speaker contends that social inequality
will persist as long as privilege is unexamined and unques-
tioned. Issues of color, class, sex, and gender collide as never be-
fore in this terse and packed eighteen-line lyric. The speaker
knows the wars. The imagery of the "mirror" and the "bed"
seem naively self-reflexive metaphors of women's oppression.
But the vehicles are also signs, as it were, which represent to the
speaker the structuring of racist, sexist, heterosexist, capitalist in-
stitutions. This poem is one of the earliest pieces of writing to
reflect the core black feminist tenet that oppression is a process
of asymmetrical simultaneity. Black feminists like Lorde and,
later, members of the Combahee River Collective in its "Black
Feminist Statement" theorized that black women and other
women of color experience oppression from multiple sources,
not solely on the basis of race. Because women, poor people,
homosexual people, for example, are all devalued in this culture,
black women, who might claim membership in each of those

aforementioned categories as well, began to find it difficult to always follow the black nationalist call to be "black first" (Lee 18).

As I have emphasized thus far, the assassination of King was a ruthless climax to an era of staunch and devout hope. As adamantly as Gwendolyn Brooks gave notice to Harper & Row, after the publication of *In the Mecca*, that her poetry would be published by Broadside Press, a noticeable signal of her turn to a black cultural nationalist poetics, Alice Walker, twenty-four, defiantly published *Once* in 1969 with Harcourt Brace Jovanovich. The manuscript, however, was written in 1965 during her sojourn in Uganda, East Africa, and her senior year at Sarah Lawrence College (*Her Blue Body Everything We Know* 3). The title, *Once*, embodies Walker's abiding literary concern with the past and its influence on the present. There is no expression in these poems of longing for the "homeland" now reclaimed, no romanticizing of African history, no self-deprecation of one's "New World" roots, and not even the naive cynicism of Cullen's "Heritage." It is a book of terse encounters with the African and southern U.S. landscapes as well as the terrain of (hetero)sexuality; and the poems "Once," "The Kiss," and "Johann" explore the heresy of interracial love and sex. In an increasingly black-identified poetry milieu, making sexual attraction to white men public or savoring one's sexual desire for a member of the "enemy ranks" over one's loyalty to one's "race" could be dangerous. The poems also depict encounters between the forces and the voices of integration and segregation, which Walker experienced first-hand as a Civil Rights worker in voter registration in Mississippi. Humor and irony gird many of these spare and sinewy statements.

However, for me one of the most interesting poems in this collection is Walker's "Ballad of the Brown Girl," which signifies on Countee Cullen's far less efficient and exceedingly more romantic poem, "The Ballad of the Brown Girl," from his 1927 book of poems of the same name. The poem is also a response to and revision of Cullen's 1925 "A Brown Girl Dead" and Hughes's 1927 "Song for a Dark Girl," both epitaphlike poems about premature death, aborted life, represented by a young black woman—as if the oppressed are feminized by their oppression. Walker's narrative, told in fifty truncated lines, is the story of a thwarted abortion and subsequent suicide. It speaks back to Cullen and Hughes that, far from being only an emblem of the race's oppression, black women suffer an oppression that is exponential because of their gender and race. The abortion is thwarted because the patronizing doctor, despite the "brown girl's" ability to pay him, counsels her to "talk it over with your folks" (136). Hanging herself in her dormitory room, the brown girl leaves a note, "cryptic" and "collegiate," that explains her preference for death than to live in her family and community as the unmarried mother of a baby whose father is white (136).

In this efficient and well-made poem, one can predict the themes that will distinguish Walker's fiction: oppression of women, wasted lives, cruelty of one's family and community, and death in defiance of unbearable life. The formalistic qualities of "Ballad of a Brown Girl" counterpoint the "Edie Bauer" segment in Brooks's "In the Mecca"; Walker's final sarcastic, ironic sing-song also tolls the death of lyric, of communal compassion, of interracial possibility. All the emphatic cries for rebirth, regeneration, rediscovery seem not to faze this young daughter of the South, who is ambivalent about the new blackness, which Brooks and many other black poets hailed as "luminously indiscreet / complete; continuous" ("The Sermon on the Warpland" 50).

Thus, in her twenty-six-line narrative, "Revolutionary Petunias" from her second volume of poems of the same title, Walker takes us to the "backwoods" (presumably the South) and gives us the poor unsung black woman heroine, "Sammy Lou of

Rue," whose "revolutionary" act causes her to lose her life. Like the previously discussed Clifton poem, "miss rosie," Sammy Lou is not a representation of black womanhood vaunted by the Black Arts Movement. She is a gardener, a single-parent (of five children), and recently widowed. She killed her husband's murderer with a "cultivator's hoe" and is moving toward the electric chair, not in "straight / / revolutionary / lines / toward some enemy" like Sonia Sanchez's brothers and sisters in "blk/rhetoric." Though never stated, we know the "creature" Sammy Lou kills is white, which, in the South, if one is black, is a death sentence. Use of the terms "angry" and "militant" locates the action in the contemporary era. The poem offers a critique of the media representations of black women activists who openly speak out or defend themselves against the violence of the state. Moreover, the poem blatantly critiques the Black Arts Movement's privileging of the urban landscape, idealized black nationalist subjects, and the romanticized revolution.

The poem has all the grit, pathos, and gothic tension of Walker's first novel, *The Third Life of Grange Copeland* and her first book of short stories, *In Love and Trouble*, and is a template for her later fiction, *Meridian*, *You Can't Keep a Good Woman Down*, and *The Color Purple*. Sammy Lou of Rue did not *rue* the day she killed "the exact creature" who murdered her husband.

Walker pays tribute to her literary godmother, Zora Neale Hurston, by presenting this salt-of-the-earth figure, Sammy Lou of Rue—much like Big Sweet in *Mules and Men* or Sophia, Celie's sister-in-law in *The Color Purple*. She also pays tribute to the Civil Rights Movement of the deep South, whose ranks were made up of just such people—Fannie Lou Hamer being one of the more well-known grassroots activists. Even Sammy Lou's name, being both male and female, signifies subversivenes. Finally, even her petunias are revolutionary. And Sammy Lou's speech is appropriately Southern, as she demands "y'all" not to forget to water her "purple petunias"—the vernacular "y'all" being constitutive of the black movement. As always, Walker works to tell a womanist story.

She continued to explore in her poetry the legacy of the Civil Rights Movement in *Revolutionary Petunias*, while black nationalist sentiments had begun to wane in the poetry of other black women poets. Malcolm X and his teachings—before and after his hadj to Mecca—were still consumed by black nationalists and many black radicals as the lessons needed to liberate black people from the moral morass and bad taste of Babylon. King, however, for Walker, remained the sign of sacrifice and atonement, major themes in her second novel, *Meridian* (1976), still one of the few novels to explore the emotional and psychic toll of the Civil Rights Movement. She addressed the fraught and freighted legacy of Malcolm X in her sentimental poem, "Malcolm," in her 1979 collection *Goodnight, Willie Lee, I'll See You In The Morning*.

A consummate outsider and also not one to suffer any fools gladly nor compromise her literary autonomy, Walker defied both orthodoxy and dogmatism—like her literary foremother, Hurston—in her poetry as well as in her fiction. *Revolutionary Petunias and Other Poems* was nominated for a National Book Award in 1973, along with Audre Lorde's *From a Land Where Other People Live* and Adrienne Rich's *Diving into the Wreck*.

Elouise Loftin is another counterpoint voice to the certitudes of the Black Arts Movement. Her work offers a post-Mecca meditation on black women's vernacular tongues. She is definitely in the "black tradition" in her use of black urban speech. In the first poem, "woman," from her first collection, *Jumbish* (1972), the speaker enunciates her role in the telling. She is a seer, a corrector, a near irreconcilable force, inevitable-seeming.

> as a child I was
> constantly reminded

of the size of my eyes
or how I just saw 'evahthing'
and was always warned
not to look into grown folks mouths (6)

From Phillis Wheatley to Alice Walker, Black women—have been constantly penalized—by black people as well as white people—for their own use of language. Loftin revises an age-old African-American admonition to black children: warning young people not to get caught up in grown people's business, to yield to the authority of adults, and not to look "grown folks" in the eye. (Sometimes that admonition allows us to proxy "white folks" for "grown folks.")

As a child of the Black Arts and the Civil Rights movements, but also a believer in women's autonomy, Loftin uses all these influences to establish her ground. Her speaker asserts her nonconformity, her subversiveness, her intention to read and interpret the culture.

somehow I find myself looking to
where i've been looking all the time
into folks mouths caught in poses
that pierce all time and distances
gaping off into space (6)

The poet seems to equate "woman" with the ability to be duplicitous, to "see you from where / you don't see me / see you." The poet claims a knowledge of the folks that the folks don't have of the poet or the child or the woman or the "I." Actually, the precocious speaker anticipates Alice Walker's creation of the signifier, "womanist," derived from "womanish," by about twelve years. Loftin's tone throughout her impressive first collection is like that of the rhythm and blues singer—that combination of innocence, passion, and vulnerability—as she sees her world and her place in it: "I want to see less pain" ("They'll Nevah Get Me" 7). "These Streets" seems to evoke the despair left of the cities in the wake of so much destruction and death in the riots between 1965 and 1970. "They have stolen my odor / and spread the smell of death / and gasoline high into my body" (8).

The third in a series of "Sunni" poems, "Sunni," closes Loftin's collection; I discussed "Sunni Unveiling" earlier in the chapter. The second poem, "what Sunni say" is a twelve-line en-jambed, existential yearning for identity: "open me up the me of me / put it inside where i need" (33). The "Sunni" who appears at the end might be one with Brooks's "Big Bessie," the citizen of the "wild weed." She searches for "old blues tunes," that is, the past, in "hidden stores." The night is her sanctuary, which she "stalks . . . in spite of warnings / with clenched fist of screaming / hot peppers for sucker fools" (40). Sunni is pro-tected by "gri gri" dust, given her by a "truth bearing poet." In the way that Hurston situated the writer (that is, herself), Loftin situates the poet (that is, herself) in a tradition of magic and two-headedness. In discussing this poem, Aldon Lynn Neilsen contends that "Loftin's text . . . links the blues and gri-gri of North American and Caribbean diasporic blacks to the cultural practices of an African past" (*Black Chant* 199).[6]

This "Sunni" is a seer who "knows no limits." The poem ends, as "Sunni's Unveiling," in the womb, but not as a site of re-generation this time but as a site of clairvoyance: "Her mother's womb had a window / so she know [sic] exactly what she / was coming into." If Sunni knew what the rest of the decade of the 1970s would bear, she, like Ben Jonson's "infant of Saguntum,"[7] might have crawled back inside her mother's womb.

The Black Arts Movement transformed black writers and a wide range of reading publics during those turbulent years of creativity, and not without leaving its mark on a generation of black women writers who moved inside and outside its circle. With the publication of *The Black Woman* in 1970, black women writers began to turn toward feminist or, as Alice Walker would

come to call years later, "womanist" values. Feminists, particu-
larly lesbian-feminists, were able to use their tools to build a
literary culture that had never before existed in the public.
However, by 1973, many of the radical/revolutionary shape-
shifters had been destroyed or imprisoned: the Black Panthers'
imploded; George Jackson was framed and murdered in the
Soledad Prison yard; Huey P. Newton was jailed; Eldridge
Cleaver had long since escaped to Algeria; Angela Davis was ac-
quitted of trumped-up murder, kidnapping, and conspiracy
charges in 1972 after sixteen months in jail and a million dollars
in legal fees; Stokely Carmichael had expatriated to Africa; H.
Rap Brown was in prison; Assata Shakur (aka Joanne Chesi-
mard), putative leader of the Black Liberation Army, was jailed
and convicted of murder in New Jersey by 1976. COINTELPRO
had wreaked havoc in the black liberation movement.[8] In 1973,
"These Are The Times" by Jayne Cortez offers a chilling
epitaph:

> These are the times of sterility
> of hormone shots and lobotomies
> of dehydrated funk and stagnated celebrities
> these are the times of solitary confinement. (*Scarifi-
> cations* 21)

Finally, black women poets "within" and "without" the cir-
cle of the Black Arts Movement spoke to the imagined black
community. They assaulted white America with their words.
They critiqued and paid homage to the dictates, the ortho-
doxies, and the enunciated desires of their black brothers and
comrades.

CHAPTER 4

Black Feminist Communalism

NTOZAKE SHANGE'S *FOR COLORED GIRLS WHO HAVE CONSIDERED SUICIDE/WHEN THE RAINBOW IS ENUF*

FROM "COLORED GIRLS" TO BLACK WOMEN

Women's participation in art and politics signaled feminist potential and presented first and foremost challenges to male dominance. Longings for a militant literacy, sexual autonomy, and a poetics not circumscribed by whiteness and maleness, fomented the beginnings of black feminist and lesbian-feminist production, circa 1973. By the early seventies lesbian feminists—mostly white, some black—were forming and joining autonomous women's organizations, institutions, businesses, and communities—some as separatists. They shared longings for "women-identified-women's" space, culture, and politics. U.S. Black, Latina, Native, and Asian lesbians embraced feminism more visibly in the mid to late seventies, as Ntozake Shange confirms in her "preface" to the Collier-MacMillan edition of the choreopoem, *for colored girls who have considered suicide/when the rainbow is enuf*, based on the Broadway production:

San Francisco was inundated with women poets, women's readings, & a multilingual women's presence, new to all of us & desperately appreciated. . . . During the same period, Shameless Hussy Press & The Oakland Women's Press Collective were also reading anywhere & everywhere they could. In a single season, Susan Griffin, Judy Grahn, Barbara Gravelle, & Alta, were promoting the poetry & presence of women in a legendary male-poet's environment. This is the energy & part of the style that nurtured *for colored girls.* . . . (*In the summer of 1974 I had begun a series of seven poems, modeled on Judy Grahn's The Common Woman.*)(xii)

In the passage above, Ntozake Shange describes her witness of the ways women's literary culture changed women's lives in the 1970s. She sees herself as both a beneficiary and an arbiter of those changes. That Shange cites the work of lesbian-feminist poet Judy Grahn and the West Coast women's independent press movement as having enabled and influenced *for colored girls who have considered suicide/when the rainbow is enuf* is striking.[1] In fact, the first edition of the "choreopoem" was published by Shameless Hussy, a women's press in San Francisco. In 1976, when this preface was written, citing an allegiance to feminist and lesbian projects was still risky for ostensibly straight black women writers. Equally striking is Shange's omission of her debt to the Black Arts Movement. (Was this not so much omission as rejection?) Shange, a black feminist, was deeply informed by black American vernacular practices, Black Arts Movement poetics, and the militant reverence for the new music and its exponents, namely, for her during this time, Coltrane, Archie Shepp, Albert Ayler—to name a very few. And like many Black Arts exponents, Shange often performed her poetry with musicians.

Shange had lived through the integrationist Civil Rights and the nationalist Black Power movements and carried their lessons to the nascent feminist projects in which she became involved. The lessons of the Black Arts Movement internalized by black lesbian feminists were internalized by white lesbian feminists as well. Judy Grahn's early work, with its white working-class poetics, learned a lot about identity and voice from the Black Arts Movement. Perhaps in this late 1970s moment by citing Judy Grahn as an influence, Shange pays tribute to her Black Arts influence (rather like paying homage to that Little Richard behind every Jerry Lee Lewis and that Big Mama Thornton behind every Elvis Presley).

Shange tells us of her debt to the Black Arts Movement in her acknowledgment of the influence of Baraka in "i talk to myself," an auto interview, prefatory to her 1979 volume of poems, *nappy edges*: "around 1966/abt the time I went to barnard I thot leroi jones (imamu baraka) was my primary jumping-off point. that I cd learn from him how to make language sing & penetrate one's soul, like in *the dead lecturer* [1964], *the system of dante's hell* [1965] & *black magic poetry* [1969]" (22–23). In addition to Baraka, she acknowledges Ishmael Reed, David Henderson, and Pedro Pietri. She does acknowledge her indebtedness to a few women, her peers, Jessica Hagedorn, Carol Lee Sanchez. She pays homage to Thulani Davis, another poet, in "things I wd say," a critical excursion into the poetry that shaped her linguistic artistry, also prefatory to the volume *nappy edges*. She does continue to give credit to the West Coast women's, poet's, artist's milieu that shaped *for colored girls*.

She was also not enamored of commercial theater, that is, Broadway, despite the commercial success of *for colored girls*, and early on she cites her opposition to the artistic compromises necessary to become a commodity (Tate, 170). Yet, I believe, in the aftermath of the hostile criticism *for colored girls* received from the black press and individual black male critics and intellectuals, Shange became anxious about her authenticity/acceptance as a black artist. She is careful to reveal her indebtedness to the fathers by the time of the publication of *nappy edges*, 1979. Also in 1979, sociologist Robert Staples's long opinion piece,

"The Myth of Black Macho: A Response to Angry Black Feminists," was featured in the May/June issue of *The Black Scholar* and captures the curious defensiveness of black men over black women writing about the sexual politics in the black community. Staples harangues against Shange as well as Michele Wallace for her provocative (though wrong-headed) book, *Black Macho and the Myth of the Superwoman* (*Black Macho*). He stops just short of calling black feminists instruments in "an all out attack on black males," orchestrated by white feminists (24). He further states: "Watching a performance [of *for colored girls*] one sees a collective appetite for black male blood" (26). (Did he mean to liken black feminists to vampires?)

In response to letters from its readership, *The Black Scholar* published, in 1979 as well, its special issue, "Reader's Forum on Black Male/Female Relationships,"[2] where a cross-section of the black intelligentsia weighed in on the hotly debated gender politics of the black community in the United States. Wallace's *Black Macho*, Shange's *for colored girls*, and Staples's piece served as the grounding texts.

Shange faired better in the "Reader's Forum" than Wallace, but *for colored girls* still took some heavy hits. Perhaps the most outlandish critique is cultural nationalist and conspiracy theorist Askia M. Toure's dismissive lumping of both *for colored girls* and *Black Macho* in with COINTELPRO and " 'blaxploitation' " films as part of the U.S. government's "assault against [black] people" (45). And perhaps the response that most misreads *for colored girls* is, interestingly enough, that of poet Sherley A. Williams, who declaims *for colored girls* "is not an anthem of female liberation but [a] dirge of defeat" (49) because Shange is guilty of the same expression of gender chauvinism of which she accuses black men.

In the previously discussed passage from Shange's 1976 introduction to *for colored girls*, she describes the communal effort of the West Coast women's movement in producing *for colored girls.* The development of *for colored girls* on the West Coast mirrors the development of community and coalition among feminists—lesbian and nonlesbian, white and women of color—all over the country, not only among black women as was depicted in the commodified Broadway version of *for colored girls.*

In its deployment of theater and music (R&B, jazz, salsa) ensemble techniques, its revision of Afro-American call and response, Afro-American folk rituals, and the pastiche of signifiers from other diaspora cultures in *for colored girls,* black women function synecdochally for women of color and indeed all women—in community—recovering their voices and stories and doing their work. As both a feminist communal project and a representation of nascent (black) feminist community, *for colored girls* changed perceptions of black women's feminist agency. On the East Coast it challenged the male-centered theater repertories—black, white, off-Broadway and on—by putting seven black women on the stage for two hours to tell a "black girl's story" in the white male–dominated world of theater where there was and is not a lot of work for black women actors. For that alone, Black Theater should be endlessly grateful to the production of *for colored girls.* I remember my own excitement upon witnessing the workshop production of *for colored girls* at the Henry Street Settlement House in New York City in 1975, prior to its Broadway run, which began in 1976. Not one who grew up in the black church, I, nonetheless, found myself constituting a one-woman Amen Corner, when the "lady in red," played in that early New York City production by the towering Trazana Beverly, exclaimed "I found god in myself / & loved her/loved her fiercely."

The first three words, "for colored girls," of the title of Shange's electrifying piece defy the prevailing nomenclature. The appellation, "colored" was cast out—even before "Negro"—of the Black Power/Black Arts cosmos as an erasure of Afro-

Americans' African roots. The designation "black" had become firmly and formally established in American culture by the time Shange had begun to develop her "choreopoem." Neither feminists nor black cultural proponents would allow the designation of "girls" for (black) women. Use of either "colored" or "girls" in public—never mind on Broadway—risks a hostile reception by black audiences. The preposition "for" resonates subversiveness, if only because it signals the directness of Shange's (or the piece's) intentions; she intends to say something to black women and/or women of color, to whom no theatre had been saying much. This form, by speaking to "colored girls," draws a circle for them and bids them enter. In his study, *Ntozake Shange: A Critical Study of the Plays*, Neal A. Lester construes that the first three words, "for colored girls" are "at once a stark reminder of humiliating Jim Crow moments in American history. 'For Colored Only' signs reminded blacks that they were not equal to whites and innately unworthy of sharing the same territorial space with whites. In much the same way, Shange's seven women reclaim their own space in their move toward realized selfhood" (24). Simultaneously, the title allows black readers (of text, theater, popular culture, etc.) to enjoy its parody of the movement's appeals to "the race" to be men. Because of Black Arts poets' ingenious deployments of black vernacular speech, discussed in the previous chapter, Shange's allusion to a past language has its nostalgic appeal to several audiences. However, its conjunction of "rainbow" and "suicide"—the other parts of Shange's mystifying title—jolts readers out of most nostalgic notions before either reading or seeing the play. (After the popularization by Judy Garland and others of "Somewhere Over the Rainbow" for over forty years, how could a "rainbow" not be en[uf]ough?) While this absurdist strategy of the conjoining of paradoxical signifiers to produce lethal effects does not find its source only in the Black Arts, the Black Arts practitioners put to creative effects in its theatre this ostensibly

European influence, and, in turn, Shange makes use of it in the appealing narratives of *for colored girls*. The text of the play is rendered in lower-case print, back slashes, and plenty of white space—like much of Black Arts poetry. Textually, the "choreopoem" can and does pass as a poem.

I would like to offer an extended reading of *for colored girls* as a composite of the Black Arts Movement literacies deployed to create a circle for black feminists to theorize community and to effect that in the symbolic making of the "choreopoem." Although I ground my reading in the Collier-Macmillan text, from time to time I turn to poems in the Shameless Hussy Press edition omitted from the Collier-Macmillan edition. Shange's *for colored girls* cleared space for more "colored girls" to tell their stories, as was and remains its (abiding) intent. However, the Broadway production of *for colored girls* sacrifices the cultural ethics that undergird the California development of this work. The Collier-Macmillan edition shows Shange in moments extending its lessons beyond the specificity of black women. The change in focus from women of color to black women is not only an accommodation of the New York theater market, which, since Jean Genet's *The Blacks*, Lorraine Hansberry's *Raisin in the Sun*, and James Baldwin's *Blues For Mister Charlie* had become accustomed to seeing black people as assertive dramatic subjects. But the "sacrifice" is also an accommodation of the Black Aesthetic, which was embedded in New York Black Theater—on and off Broadway. In the interview with Claudia Tate in *Black Women Writers At Work*, Shange provides insight into the development of her multicultural feminist roots: "We met together in groups by ourselves: black, white, Asian, and Native-American women. We did our work for our own people, and all of my work just grew from there" (174).

Shange works with the irony of giving her characters no name but "lady," a designation of gentility historically denied black women and whose application to any women now is most dubious unless as irony. The ladies' anonymity creates a communalism and commonality of experience. They are black "everywomen." Critique and homage are embedded in their identities. *[F]or colored girls* is a coming of age and semi-autobiographical piece projected onto a generation of sexually liberated black women who came of age during the 1960s—aspiring, educated, politically active, artistic, and ostensibly heterosexual; women, who were now living out the race, sex, and gender contradictions of the era. The geography of its daughters from "outside chicago . . . . detroit . . . . houston. . . . baltimore . . . . san francisco . . . . st. louis . . . ." (5) mirrors the author's own geography. Born Paulette Williams in Trenton, New Jersey, in 1948, Shange changed her name in 1971, while a graduate student at UCLA; in Zulu, "Ntozake" means "she who comes with her own things," and "Shange" means "who walks like a lion."

Further, the ladies of *for colored girls* talk to each other and turn their circle out. The "lady in brown" serves, according to P. Jane Splawn, as an interlocutor and an interpreter throughout the performance. She opens and closes the piece and sometimes explains the action and utterances. Opening, she decries the erasure of "a black girl's song," her spiritual dying, and the marginalization of her cultural significance. Yet, as the cultural midwife, "lady in brown" asks for "the black girl" to be born "& handled warmly." The black children's games, "mama's little baby loves shortnin bread" and "little sally walker" signal the exclusiveness of the circle of colored girls by relocating the ritual from the black folk milieu to the milieu of the stage. This "milieu" is *their* game.

Dancing and R&B translate the longings for sexual experience. Strains of "Stay," a lyrical song of sexual desire and vulnerability recorded in the late fifties by the classic doo-wop group, The Dells, is played alternately during "lady in yellow's" rap on sexual knowledge (8).

Shange's ladies are committed to minds and spirits. Fantasy, dreaming, imagining, conjuring as well as thinking are privileged throughout the choreopoem, for they signify women's psychic liberation. Because "lady in yellow" fantasizes about her own sexual fulfillment in the lines above, she takes control of her sexuality and experiences losing her virginity as a necessary rite of passage—and not unpleasant.

"WE WAZ GROWN" is a resonant pronouncement among U.S. black women, as suggested in the previous chapter about Elouise Loftin's poem, "woman." Black women are told from the first time we ask adults about sex that we have to be "GROWN"—and preferably married. In the Shange lexicon, "GROWN" also means "free." Shortly, the ladies will tell about the downside of "GROWN."

A quick repartée among the ladies in red, blue, and yellow (performed by Shange in the Henry Street Settlement House and Broadway versions) introduces the narrative of a more sophisticated subject who wants to move beyond the end of her rainbow to the South Bronx to "meet up with willie colon." No parochial "grind," disdained by the lady in blue in the previous scene, but now says lady in blue, "mambo, bomba, merengue." Shange's project is to know black culture in diaspora, to make connections, to create disruption, to recover the stories, to revise the narrative, "to sing a black girl's song" (4) even as that black girl is, as "lady in blue" says, "a mute cute colored puerto rican."

Blackness, that is, "alla my niggah blood," will not be denied and is unsparing in its tutelage. "Blackness," as learned from the Black Arts Movement, is that essential critique of racial hybridity, cultural contamination, and sexual autonomy. Blackness makes "lady in blue" recall an earlier literacy attained by "sneaking under age into slug's" (13), a famous lower east side jazz club of the 1960s where avant gardists and experimentalists like John Coltrane, Ornette Coleman, Pharoah Sanders, Archie Shepp, and others, including icons like Amiri Baraka, performed: "imamu's mouth was gospel" (13). The jazz club, while regarded as a secular venue, is also a sacred space of black culture since early described in James Weldon Johnson's *The Autobiography of an Ex-Colored Man* (1912)[3]—and so it remained, for generations of black people into the sixties era of Afro-American reinvention. Shange invokes and yokes sacred and profane blackness: "if jesus cdnt play a horn like shepp / waznt no need for colored folks to bear the cross at all" (13).

Poetry is once again put to the task of making an idol of black music and found wanting. However, while her poetic debt to "imamu" is clear, Shange also owes a serious debt to black women poets. The above cited lines signify on lines from Nikki Giovanni's "Poem for Aretha," namely, "if she [aretha] had said 'come / let's do it' it would have been done" (Brooks, ed. 63). In the "te amo mas que" sequence, "lady in blue's" narrative of experience dissolves into a paean to Afro-American and Afro-Latino musical icons Billie Holiday ("lady"), Celia Cruz ("celia"), and the late fifties, early sixties doo-wop group, the Flamingoes. For Shange's "colored girls," the primary transmitters of black culture are black or Latino singers and musicians, often men (The Dells, The Flamingoes, Willie Colon, Archie Shepp, The Art Ensemble of Chicago), except for "billie . . . celia . . . graciela." The invocation, "oyè négro," may even be a nostalgic appeal to the notion that the "race" needed to be masculinized. Oyè négr*a*!

To the "lady in blue's" unqualified "love" of music—"more than poem"—"lady in red" offers a blunt counternarrative, addressed to an ungendered "you" and does not wish to search for hyperbole in Spanish to reify love. This testimony by "lady in red" is the only ungendered signifying on trifling lovers. Her articulation of a precise recollection of how she extended herself "to snare a possible lover" (14) culminates in a grand pronouncement that this excursion "waz an experiment," much like "lady in blue's" forays into the jazz club. "Lady in red's" lines burst and contract like a parodic Archie Shepp solo (14).

Sexual experimentation characterized the coming of age of postmodern black women. The term "lover" is always a code for the unconventional liaison and is markedly sexual. Whoever the lover is, "lady in red" rejects "debasin my self for the love of another" and realizes that a person who cannot water her own plant can't be trusted to maintain a relationship.

"Lady in orange" rejects English or Spanish literacy for music and dance. All the ladies dance to Willie Colon's record, "Che Che Cole." "Lady in yellow" reprises the old R&B lick, "we gotta dance to keep from cryin," and "lady in brown" reprises it with the exception of the last word, for which she substitutes "dyin." The dance and the ability to dance have been survival rituals not only for the lovelorn but for the black dispossessed, those suffering from the "missed love" Jones/Baraka speaks of in "The Changing Same." "Lady in orange" instructs the dancers and the audience to hold their heads like "it was / ruby sapphire" (16) and announces her intention to be a poet who writes in "english . . . come to share the world wichu." Not easily colonized by the poet, the ladies offer back the dance to "lady in orange" and the audience, "baya" (16).

The first part of the choreopoem ends with a communitarian call and an insistence upon a multilingual affront to any centrality—be it language, music, choreography, or geography—except "blackness." Poetry, music, dance continue to contend for space on the stage as the light changes and the ladies, reacting as if struck in their faces, take their spaces for the next choreopoem on the genealogy of rape. Rape is regarded as the just desserts of women too sexually liberated. The ladies in red, purple, and blue trade lick-like lines on the contradictions of being raped by a friend as opposed to a stranger. The earlier section on graduation night hints of the dangers posed to women intent upon sexual expression and experimentation. Speaking in the collective voices of rape survivors, the three ladies document the risks women take to control their lives. This whole sequence is striking because it meditates mainly on the dissolution of the binaries, friend and rapist:

> *lady in blue*
> a friend is hard to press charges against
>
> *lady in red*
> if you know him
>
> you must have wanted it
>
> *lady in purple*
> wit closed mouth
>
> *lady in blue*
> pressin charges will be as hard
>
> as keepin yr legs closed
>
> while five fools try to run a train on you (17)

More than any contemporary writing on the issue, this blistering sequence of casual literalness epitomizes the feminist discourse that broke the silence around sexual violence against women—and indeed all violence against women. It is one of the earliest theorizings on what we now call "date rape." The oppressive "justice" women rape survivors receive is deftly compared to gang rape in "lady in blue's" culminating lines, almost as if the only metaphor for rape is rape, as those lines drive home the lesson that enduring the aftermath of pressing rape charges is like being raped again. This sequence does not appear in the Shameless Hussy Press edition. Shange is clearly intent upon using the New York stage to give public voice to the level of violence from men and men's systems with which women must contend daily. Again, particularity is evaded. Though gendered, of course, the rapist is not *raced* or *classed*. Rapists are no respecters of race or class privilege; and they are of all races and classes—and so are the survivors. "Lady in red" ends this set with the rude irony that one's own house cannot even protect one from the "friend" invited over for dinner who is a rapist (21).

for colored girls dramatizes/performs community and insists to its audience upon a solidarity around the particularity of rape as a hallmark of women's oppression. Previously, I had questioned whether black women poets of the Black Arts Movement era were in dialogue with one another. Their collective work, in retrospect, enabled writers like Shange to imagine a black women's artistic community. Shange turns the circle in, and the ladies signify to each other. She, then, turns the circle out, disrupts it, sends them spiraling "off up left," "out the right volm," "out up right," frantically seeking other stories, other voices to testify to "we cd even . . . get raped in our own houses" (22). Is rape the only price a woman may have to pay to be sexually liberated?

After trading imagistic riffs with "lady in blue"—"eyes," "mice," "womb," "nobody"—"the lady" in purple leaves the stage, and "the lady in blue" moves to a solo on abortion by. In 1973, the U.S. Supreme Court ruled, in *Roe v. Wade* and *Doe v. Bolton*, that the constitutional right of privacy includes the right of a woman to decide whether or not to terminate her pregnancy. "Lady in blue's" sequence on abortion is as compelling as Brooks's 1945 poem, "the mother" (*A Street in Bronzeville*) and Alice Walker's 1965 poem, "Ballad of a Brown Girl" (*Once*) both of which deal with abortion pre-*Roe v. Wade*. "Lady in blue's" story is not necessarily meant to be pre-*Roe v. Wade*, but, in any event, it reflects a woman's emotional and psychic trauma of the experience, the loneliness of the secrecy, and the possibility of serious injury or death, which may result from this strictly female experience.

In his article, "Shange's Men: For Colored Girls Revisited, and Movement Beyond," Neal A. Lester argues persuasively against the still prevailing ideology that Shange leads the radical feminist pack in a "desire for black male blood" (Staples). He reads her male characters, in both *for colored girls* and *a photograph: lovers in motion*, as complex creations who have also suffered at the hands of "patriarchy," yet who are still responsible for the abuses they inflict upon black women. He uses the abortion narrative as a chief example of how Shange maintains a balanced perspective of the historical baggage carried by black men and black women: "Even the poem about abortion . . . is not a comment on some male's doing a female wrong. . . . Instead, it is an indictment of a society of men and women that ostracizes women who celebrate their sexuality freely, a society that makes a woman's biology her destiny of shame" (321). I add that this story indicts a society that polices women and punishes legally and emotionally those who take control of their bodies. Also, this story critiques a society in which unmarried mothers are scorned by the same forces who rail against abortion, as "lady in blue" declaims: "i cdnt have people / lookin at me / pregnant" (22).

As a theater piece, poem, ritual/rite for black women to recover their stories, *for colored girls* functions synecdochally for "the rites of passage experienced by New World people in the diaspora" (Splawn 391). Yes! In homage to the Black Arts protocol of myth revision, Shange presents "lady in purple" to tell the story of "Sechita" (little dry one), the "creole carnival" side show exotic dancer, who has seen better (and younger) days, "had learned to make allowances for the distortions" (24). In *Workings of the Spirit: The Poetics of Afro-American Women's Writing*, Houston A. Baker terms the "Sechita" interlude "the temporal image," and, as such, it eludes definition and is "both an imagined event and an event energized through the reading, performance, or participation demanded by its intersubjectivity" (169). It is one of several such interventions in *for colored girls*, during which a myth is created or revised.

Though I prefer the term "intervention," for in it action and instability are implicit, I subscribe to Baker's notion of the "temporal image" as "transitional." "Intervention" seems less fixed than "image." "Lady in green" enters and dances out Sechita's life to "lady in purple's" narration. Through the dance and story, Shange transports us to gritty Natchez, Mississippi, where Sechita, at the turn of the previous century, longs for the "store bought" grime of St. Louis, signifying on the lyrics of W. C. Handy's popular and popularized "St. Louis Blues." Performing this minstrel ritual to "red-neck whoops n slapping on the back," Sechita nonetheless imagines herself an "egyptian / goddess of creativity / 2nd millenium . . . nefertiti / approachin her own tomb. . . . goddess / of love / egypt" as her legs slash "furiously thru the cracker night" (25).

"Sechita," like the personae of Giovanni's "ego trippin" and Evans's "I am a Black Woman," imagines herself larger than life, but unstable and in more immediate danger than Giovanni's and Evans's nostalgic and glorified black women. Sechita's fantasy enables her to subvert the racist/misogynist venue of the nineteenth-century minstrel show, sexual spectatorship, and the (white) male objectifying gaze. Fantasy enables possibility and creativity as well as versatility and survival. It enables agency: "sechita / . . . kicked viciously / thru the nite / catchin stars tween her toes."

"Lady in brown," interlocutor and "confidence woman" (Splawn 389), returns to spin a fable of fantasy and literacy. The story of "TOUSSAINT L'OUVERTURE/JONES" revises Frederick Douglass's 1848 narrative of literacy. A seven-year-old precocious girl finds herself in the adult reading room of a St. Louis library. Disdained by adults for her resistance to reading children's books, she is disqualified from winning a contest for the "colored child who can read / 15 books in three weeks" (26), because she "raved abt TOUSSAINT L'OUVERTURE." Douglass, of course, is forbidden to learn to read anything because, as his master decries and decrees, "learning unfits a man to be a slave." Just as Douglass continues to pursue literacy as that "pathway from slavery to freedom," the girl continues to teach herself about the Haitian revolutionary who threw off the shackles of slavery in the eighteenth century. This narrative is also another example of Shange's insistence on pursuing literacy of blackness beyond the boundaries of the United States. Shange boasts of her own transcendent literacy in a 1989 taped interview: "I am everywhere they took a slave in the new world. I speak all those languages. I am all those people" (Bonetti).

In attaining this literacy of blackness/history, the girl learns to fantasize a relationship with TOUSSAINT and to develop a dissatisfaction with her "integrated home," "integrated street," "integrated school" (27), stating that "1955 waz not a good year for lil blk girls." Then, "Toussaint said 'lets go to haiti.'"

By 1955, the Supreme Court had ruled in *Brown vs. the Board of Education of Topeka, Kansas* that segregation of public schools was unconstitutional and ordered integration of public schools to proceed "with all deliberate speed." That same year, Rosa Parks was arrested for refusing to yield her bus seat to a white man in Montgomery, Alabama. Emmett Till, a fourteen-year-old boy from Chicago, was murdered in LeFlore County, Mississippi, for allegedly whistling at a white woman. These three events alone are enough to cause the girl to make the claim that it was not a good year for little black girls.

However, during the course of running away with her imagined "secret lover," confidant, and strategist, TOUSSAINT L'OUVERTURE, the girl encounters a real boy named "'TOUSSAINT JONES,'" for whom she decides to throw over the fantasy of "TOUSSAINT L'OUVERTURE." "TOUSSAINT JONES," like his revolutionary namesake, "don't take no stuff from no white folks" (30) either. And the two become comrades, for they will have their own "haiti" to free in the coming years: "toussaint jones waz awright with me."

This fable is intended to posit a retrospective vision of gender equality in the context of the struggle against racism, not an

inane valorization of female heterosexuality. Also, it is a lesson
that recovering one's past may lead to discovering one's rela-
tionship to the present, a relationship of struggle. Like the Black
Arts Movement women poets, Shange's political mentors tend
to be men—Malcolm X, Martin Luther King, Patrice Lu-
mumba, Hannibal, and now "TOUSSAINT." "I am an absolute
exponent of my people's heritage," Shange again swears her al-
legiance to black culture (Bonetti).

"Lady in red" introduces the next choreopoem: of the
"sullen," sexually liberated, self-reflexive "passion flower of
southwest/los angeles" with "orange butterflies & aqua sequins
ensconsed tween slight bosoms." This intervention like the "se-
chita" segment works to create a feminist mythology of black
women's sexual agency. Like "sechita," "passion flower" is exhi-
bitionistic, versatile, and carnal: "she waz hot / a deliberate co-
quette / who never did without / what she wanted" (32).

"Lady in red" elaborates upon what it means to be "a delib-
erate coquette," that is, "a wound . . . to every man/arragant [sic]
enough to want her." "Passion flower" is concerned with sur-
faces—those that conceal her guerilla intentions. She defies
men by reversing the roles and rules of (hetero)sexual politics,
by assuming a dominance. She controls her body even as "she
kissed / them [men] reverently . . . even ankles / edges of
beards" (33). In a postcoital decentering of the man in her bed,
"passion flower" discards her coquette surface:

> ordinary
> brown braided woman
> with big legs & full lips
> reglar
> seriously intendin to finish her
> night's work. (34)

Here Shange presents an allegory of refusal by applying the
lesson of "lady in red's" previous narrative," "without any assis-

tance from you." Lady in red's "reglar" colored girl joins with the "lady in blue's" previously discussed "mute cute colored puerto rican" in her expression of "alla my niggah."[4] The mask of "passion flower" evaporates before her visitor's eyes when the "reglar colored girl" asks her visitor: "why don't you go home" (34). "Alla my niggah" and "reglar" (colored girl) are for Shange that same essential blackness and resistance. Rejection of male and of white/Western definitions at every turn is crucial to Shange's (feminist) project, to write women into the race, a tedious and thankless project, sometimes mediated only by one's ability to deploy brilliant images of light and touch, as in the final part of "lady in red's" confession: "she placed the rose behind her ear / & cried herself to sleep."

As if to proclaim to the world (of the audience) from the beginning that the "colored girls" are in control of sexual exchange here, "Orange butterflies and aqua sequins," entitled "one," opens the Shameless Hussy Press edition instead of the "dark phases of womanhood" narration that opens the Collier-Macmillan edition. Coming after the Toussaint segment as it does in the Collier-Macmillan edition, this temporal intervention of the adult woman who has mastered a kind of sexual literacy through fantasy is juxtaposed to the woman-child who masters historical literacy through fantasy: "I build fantasies that you can walk into," says Shange (Bonetti).

The next segment offers no space for fantasy or dreaming, only a "universe" of "six blocks" called "HARLEM" and only memories that liken the Pacific to "waters ancient from accra / tunis" (36). The "HARLEM" Shange exposes here is in stark contrast to the putative "New Negro" days, when her literary forebears, Langston Hughes and Zora Neale Hurston, ran the streets between rent parties and literary readings. This segment more than any marks transition *of for colored girls* from a West Coast project to an East Coast commodity, and, as well, the segment marks Shange's grief at the loss of artistic autonomy and community, as "lady in blue" laments the living alone and hints at the danger of being "a woman in the world": "i useta live in the world / now i live in harlem & my universe is six / blocks. . . . i come in at dusk / stay close to the curb" (37).

This Harlem of the 1970s is a painful ruin without the possibility of reclamation, like The Mecca building in Chicago, whose ghost was revived by Gwendolyn Brooks. This segment is a memorial to that lost possibility, that "missed love." The East Coast urban landscape is as encompassing as an ocean and more confining, and more dangerous. It is a man's world, where "tall short black brown young" men full of their power haunt the sidewalks and mean women no good.

While "lady in blue" exhorts the audience, "lady in yellow" and "lady in purple" enter on stage and pose as if waiting for a bus. Then "lady in orange" enters, and she is followed by "lady in blue," who poses as a man, miming the specific threat to women traversing the (urban) street. Though a woman can't "be nice to nobody" in this concrete desert, verbal acuity is a necessary survival strategy:

'I SPENT MORE MONEY YESTERDAY
THAN THE DAY BEFORE & ALL THAT'S MORE N
YOU
NIGGAH EVER GOTTA HOLD TO' (38)

The interior quotation marks indicate that "lady in blue" is rehearsing the signifying retort used by women to fend off would-be johns. The capitalization signifies that the speaker ("lady in blue") is *reading* the man who offers her "$5" for a sexual favor.[5] Occasionally, one can rely on the kindness of strangers who intervene with "dont pay him no mind," and who urgently advise, "go go go go go go sister"—the six repetitions emphasizing the futility of a woman standing her ground against a man on these "six blocks of cruelty / piled up on itself / a tunnel / closin" (39).

The next sequence of five poems takes the audience on a consciousness-raising excursion. Like a musical jam session, the "ladies in blue, purple, yellow, and orange" each take a solo on the cruelty of (male) lovers. "Lady in purple" tells the story of three friends, "like a pyramid," who all want the same man, who chooses one and tries to seduce the other two, "when the one who loved him waz somewhere else" (40). They choose their friendship over his "irregular" appearances and realize "how much love stood between them . . . love like sisters" (42). This poem appears in the Shameless Hussy Press edition in seventeen parts, entitled "three," and also explores the issue of male infidelity. In the Shameless Hussy edition, the "love like sisters" is specified so as to dispel assumptions that women turn to lesbianism because men are faithless, in the Collier-MacMillan edition, "love like sisters" works to dispel lesbianism for any reason.

The next solo is offered by "lady in orange" in which she eulogizes her faded love: "so this is a requiem for myself." Having refused to live out a stereotype of a "colored girl" as "an evil woman a bitch or a nag," or to be bitter, she brings her lover "what joy [she] found." Her ability to bring joy does not protect her heart from being put "in the bottom of [his] shoe," when he leaves her to return to a previous lover. Nor does her refusal to feel sorrow protect her from her "own face wet wit my tears / cuz i had convinced myself colored girls had no right to sorrow." She kicks "sorrow" to the curb, ostensibly to distance from the trifling lover, but ultimately to distance herself from her own sorrow. "Lady in orange" finally refuses the eulogy, to yoke "sorry" and "colored" onto the same body, for "it's so redundant in the modern world." In this humorous last observation about the lack of space for feeling in the modern world, she equates "sorry" and "colored" and chooses "bein . . . colored" to "bein sorry " (43).

"Lady in purple" returns with a testimonial of vulnerability and desire, as if in answer to "lady in orange's" previous testimony about sorrow. She refuses to deny her pain in sufferance to the myths and stereotypes of black women's invincibility. At one time, she allowed dance and music, which, in Shange, are codes for sexual expression and experimentation, to distract desire, saying "and music waz my ol man." However, "the baddest muthafuckah / out there" takes music's place, and not without a heavy toll, for which even dance and music can't compensate. "Lady in purple" asserts her right to allow "colored" and "sorry" to coalesce, in opposition to lady in orange, who refuses: "i am colored & really sad sometime & you hurt me / more than i ever danced outta" (44).

In the final poem of this sequence, "lady in yellow" celebrates "bein alive & bein a woman & bein colored" as a "metaphysical dilemma / i havent conquered yet," that is not transparent, not easily understood by those who cause emotional hurt, and complicated beyond the body. She admits she survives on "intimacy and tomorrow," that she is an ancient spirit who refuses to have her soul "separated" from her gender. Shange here theorizes on the permeability of the body and the emotions, that is, to be "really colored & really sad;" and thus, the impossibility of being "immune" to hurt or "impervious to pain." Finally, "lady in yellow" testifies to her realization that her "love is too delicate to have thrown back on [her] face." She repeats it, this time as an assertion, and the "ladies in brown, purple, blue, orange, red, and green" come to the realization of their worth. Each announces that her love is: "too beautiful . . . . too sanctified . . . too magic. . . . too Saturday nite. . . . too complicated. . . .too music. . . . to have thrown back on [her] face" (46–47).

This series of enunciations is each woman's elaboration of the "metaphysical dilemma" of being "alive & bein a woman & bein colored." Led by "lady in yellow," who was absent from the previous sequence, everyone repeats each descriptive word three times, except for "complicated" which is repeated eight times, until the scene culminates in a dance of frenzied collectivity and all the ladies fall out tired but full of life. Yes, "complicated."

"Lady in green's" testimony of "somebody almost walked off wid alla my stuff" is one of the most noted poems in *for colored girls*, for its insistent address. "Stuff" is Afro-American argot for one's sexuality. In black male culture "stuff" is one's genitals. And within black lesbian culture "stuff" is one's lover. Shange's punning heightens the sexual allusiveness of this passage. "Soul" cannot be separated from "gender" here. Emotions have a body. This signifying poem catches the dubious lover, "mr louisiana hot link," in the act of theft: "somebody almost run off wit alla my stuff / & i waz / standin . . . . & it wazn't a spirit took my stuff / waz a man . . . . waz a lover . . . . almost run off wit alla my stuff /" (50–51).

The theft is less a trope than a burglary. Instead of furniture, "lady in green" names body parts among the stolen items she wants returned: "arm wit hot iron scar & my leg wit the flea bite . . . my callused feet & quik language back in my mouth." The theft of linguistic desire is as crucial as the theft of sexual desire.

To render the urgency of the moment, Shange makes use of "combat breath," a concept she borrows from Frantz Fanon, Martiniquan psychiatrist and theorist of the colonized. The density of this poem on the page is unrelenting, with long lines alternating between twelve and sixteen syllables. The pauses, indicated by Shange's frequent use of front slashes, are abrupt and irregular, and there is the sense that the speaker is "responding to the involuntary constrictions and amputations of [her] humanity / in the context of combat breathing" (*See No Evil* 22), "having to be continually ready to die" (Bonetti). As in the previous poems on male infidelity and betrayal, women have to be continually ready to do battle to prevent their spirits and bodies from being killed while living in a man's world.

Sometimes the only acknowledgment of the exploitation is
"'i'm sorry,'" harps "lady in blue" (51). Then all of the ladies
improvise on a major male theme of "'i'm sorry.'" "Lady in
blue" comes back to render an extended testimony of how
"sorry" is not her baggage anymore, and that she will post a
sign, leave a message reading: "'if you called / to say yr sorry /
call somebody / else / i don't use em anymore'" (53).

This is a most triumphant piece because "lady in blue" can
admit she took the risk to "love," to be "open on purpose," and
to still "crave vulnerability & close talk," in spite of the "beatin"
her emotions took. Her final taunt suggests that the pain the
lover caused is an essential male quality: "hey man . . . steada
bein sorry alla the time / enjoy being yrself" (54). One wonders
if the "alla my stuff" and the "sorry" sequences might be exam-
ples of what Robert Staples saw as the "colored girls" appetite
for black male blood? But who says these "jive" dudes are black?
Shange does not *race* the trifling lovers in this sequence. Much
like rapists, philanderers come in all races and genders.

Some have seen "beau willie brown's" dropping his two
children from a fifth-story window, while a helpless "crystal"
looks on, as Ntozake Shange's signature characterization of
black men. "beau willie brown" is a violent, abusive, deceptive,
and irresponsible man of color. He is misdirected and has noth-
ing to offer "crystal" but destruction (Lester 319).

The struggle an audience wages with the "lady in red's"
story of "crystal" and "beau willie brown" is to receive it as one
of the many offered in *for colored girls*—not a culmination or a
resolution or an ending—but rather a terrible, gothic story of
the long battle we have still to wage against misogyny. This vio-
lence is not a myth. I call this sequence "gothic" because of
crystal's and the narrative's confinement and because, like Mor-
rison's *Beloved*, it is a story not to be passed on or retold or re-
played. Rather like the "ha'nt" (ghost) in Afro-American
culture, "lady in red's" narrative of intraracial violence and mur-

der carried out in the contested space of "crystal's" rooms is present but not seen, acknowledged, or talked about outside the rooms. This narrative as well as many of the previous stories of men who are "shallow, inconsiderate, and either incapable of communicating or unwilling to communicate except through sex, violence, or other abuse" (Lester) constitute Shange's sharpest departures from the prescriptions of the Black Arts Movement. "Show the race," especially black men, in a good light was consummately violated in "lady in red's" volatile and painful final solo.

I read this tale much like Alice Walker's 1970 novel, *The Third Life of Grange Copeland*, a genealogy of intraracial misogyny. People who have least are more endangered in those "six blocks of cruelty / piled up on itself / a tunnel / closin" (39). Racial and economic injustice stunt/warp the "soul" and "gender" of everyone they assault—not just the "beau willies" and "crystals." Therefore, I would like to read this not as a summation of Shange's vision of love between black women and black men, but rather as a theorizing on how the black community is endangered by male dominance.

Like most abusers, "beau willie" becomes more perverse in his methods of controlling "crystal." Shange creates of context for "beau willie" by acknowledging him as one of the many down-and-out Vietnam veterans, whom the United States stigmatized and ignored once they came home from that much contested war. "Crystal" was only thirteen when "beau willie . . . . caught her on the stairway" (55), and she was twenty-two when she threw him out allegedly for an infidelity (56).

"Lady in red," however, tells a collateral tale of "crystal's" struggle for autonomy, of how, after eight years of abuse and neglect, she no longer wants marriage and finally gets the notorious "order of protection," which "beau willie" violates, gains entry to their apartment, and commits the murder of the two children, whom he cajoles away from "crystal." Ironically and perversely he cruelly demands "crystal" to choose between marrying him or the deaths of her children: "he kicked the screen outta the window / & held the kids offa the sill / you gonna marry me" (59). Once again we experience the "combat breath" as we listen to "lady in red's" narration.

This story is merely a rehearsal for the still all-too-common occurrences in the lives of women, of all classes, races, sexualities. They have always been more commonplace than we assumed. In 1975, when *for colored girls* was first produced on the East Coast, one might have been able to argue that the "beau willie browns" were abberations because their stories were more rarely told. Today, the "beau willie brown" stories are legion, stories of battering, stalking, kidnaping, and murder of women, particularly those who resist men's dominance. Men also murder women's children. And, as Shange told us in her 1992 theatre piece, *Love Space Demands*, in which a crack-addicted mother sells her daughter for money to buy drugs, so do women.

"Lady in red" shifts between the voices of "beau willie" and "crystal" with fluidity and fluency by blurring the line between narrator and character, asserting control over the story in the same way "crystal" seemed to take control of her life: "o no i wdnt marry yr pitiful black ass for / nothin" (57). The rest is theater history. "Crystal's" warped trust leads to the final seduction and betrayal by "beau willie brown," "a laughin & a giggling / a hootin & a hollerin" and calling "crystal" "bitch" as he suspends the children from the fifth-floor window. Unlike any other "ladies," who never remove the distance between themselves as narrators and their subjects, "lady in red . . . . removes her mask of third-person narration" and exposes herself as "crystal" (Splawn 390).

Perhaps this "i" again functions synedochally for all the ladies who "stop short of exposing themselves" as the subjects of their own stories, especially one so horrific as "crystal's"; or perhaps Shange is saying every black woman has a "nightmarish story of male obsession" or aggression to tell. These stories are deadly critiques of compulsory heterosexuality.

The final sequence of dialogue among the "ladies" is a ritual of healing, "a layin on of hands," which had been missing from their lives. The laying on of hands traditionally occurs after some tragedy, as friends and family embrace and hold one another close to allay the sorrow and the pain. The laying on of hands is a restorative gesture. Here, the ritual is for "colored girls," after the myriad acts of unkindness from the world of men, a turning to self as an act of love. "[A] layin on of hands / the holiness of myself released" (62). "Lady in purple," who has rarely spoken, reprises the chant. Self-knowledge is as crucial to one's feminism as it is to one's blackness.

Again "lady in red" speaks of a splitting, this time a splitting that is regeneration, not of others, not of culture, not of race, but of self and the "god" in self. She utters the most memorable line in the piece, which became the warrior shout of black feminism: "I found god in myself / & i loved her/i loved her fiercely" (63). Yet, does "lady in red's" "warrior shout" function individualistically or synecdochally? The stage directions tell us: "*All of the ladies repeat to themselves softly the lines 'i found god in myself & I loved her.' It soon becomes a song of joy, started by the lady in blue. The ladies sing first to each other, then gradually to the audience. After the song peaks the ladies enter into a closed tight circle*" (64).

The interlocutor, "lady in brown," speaks from the circle this time, instead of from a position outside as she was in the beginning. She gives up her role as "interlocutor," interpreter, translator, and finally is within a tight "closed" circle as she revises and reprises her earlier line. Her first enunciation of the subject of the address, "for colored girls who have considered suicide / but moved to the ends of their own rainbows" seems a homage to black women's history of endurance and uplift. Yet, for the specific generation of colored girls represented in the choreopoem, it speaks to the need not to defer dreams and dreaming, sexuality, creativity, and knowledge. In her final enunciation, "lady in brown" offers indeterminacy in her deployment of the progressive verbal: "this is for colored girls who have considered / suicide / but are movin to the ends of their own rainbows." Colored girls are still "movin" in a way that subverts the notion of "ends." The rainbow's end is as illusive as the rainbow itself.

In a recent critical work on black women's writing, *Moorings and Metaphors*, Karla F. C. Holloway differentiates black women writers' struggles to position their black women characters within a community, a heritage, a legacy, a culture, a tradition from the struggles of black male writers; they appreciate that each category is freighted with its own contaminated history. Deploying Black Arts literacies, especially in her experimentation with writing, performance, and language, Shange illuminates a signifying space of community for the writers and for those who read them. Along with her fiction-writing sisters—Toni Morrison, Alice Walker, Gayl Jones, Toni Cade Bambara—Ntozake Shange opened a large field for the black feminist critical projects as well that ensued in the 1980s. Her vision of black women's community gave voice to the guerilla innovations of black lesbian feminist writers, who wrote themselves into that community of Afro-American women writers.

CHAPTER 5

Transferences and Confluences

BLACK ARTS AND BLACK LESBIAN-FEMINISM IN AUDRE LORDE'S *THE BLACK UNICORN*

AUDRE LORDE'S 1977 essay, "Poetry Is Not a Luxury," meditates on poetry as the language of women's deepest emotion, power, and creativity.[1] Written in 1978 in the same vein as her later essay, "The Uses of the Erotic as Power," and appearing in the same collection, *Sister Outsider*, this essay venerates poetry (and women) as the source of "true knowledge" and "lasting action" (37). Lorde sees poetry as a "dark" and "hidden" resource—much like the erotic and much like Shange's "alla my niggah blood"—women carry within themselves that will utlimately enable them to liberate themselves. Lorde never says how, for she is a visionary and oracular.[2] Lorde had learned the lessons of collective struggle through her own experiences in segments of the Civil Rights and Black Power movements, mostly in university settings. She witnessed white feminists finding voice and deploying for women's liberation many of the same tactics of struggle deployed in the Civil Rights and Black Power movements. And her work was fostered by a black literary revolution to which poetry had been instrumental. Remember, in 1973 Broadside Press published her third book of poems, *From a Land Where Other People Live,* which won a

National Book Award nomination. For Lorde, cultural literacy and recovery are essential to any political movement. She transferred these strategies and loyalties to progressive women's groups, where growing multicultural communities of feminists, especially lesbians, were beginning to use the power of collective organizing to build institutions, especially cultural venues. She applied her visions to what was already happening, citing poetry as a "vital necessity of our existence," that transforms language into "more tangible action" (37).

Women believed Lorde's black, lesbian, feminist vision of such indeterminacies as "more tangible action," for we were acting. Black Arts Movement poets and black lesbian feminist poets advocated artistic development autonomous from that "grey, hideous space," the white (masculinist and heterosexist) West. Both movements paid homage to what Wahneema Lubiano calls a "plural, fexible, and contested" (radical) black nationalism. As black lesbian-feminists, we had learned (within the various social justice movements of the nineteen sixties) to invent our political identities and histories; articulate a "belonging," connection, and solidarity with lesbians of all colors as well as black communities; construct "a utopian narrative;" adapt a cultural logic that intersected with gender, sexuality, and class politics; and enunciate an antiheterosexist analysis of white, male, and capitalist domination (232–233).[3] Where the Black Arts Movement had deferred to the new music, black feminists and lesbian feminists reclaimed past black women writers like Zora Neale Hurston, Nella Larsen, Alice Dunbar Nelson, and exalted contemporary black women fiction writers, such as Alice Walker and Toni Morrison. Lorde like novelist Toni Morrison, however, claimed no black literary lineage, only her Caribbean parentage, her Harlem roots, and her mythic foremothers, the Amazons of Dahomey. The ritual rejection of all manner of patriarchal narratives was as crucial to black feminists as rejection of the "Western [white] aesthetic" was to Black Arts

Movement practitioners. Recovering and revising the work and words of black women were cherished cultural and scholarly pursuits.

BLACK POETRY AND
LESBIAN-FEMINISM

I am not a lesbian but
I would like to have a real
experience with a girl who
is. What should I do? (Jordan 152)

Entitled "From the Talking Back of Miss Valentine Jones, No. 2," this is the second in a sequence of two June Jordan poems that pose as an advice column. Talking back, Miss Valentine Jones counsels, "Jesus is the answer. / Join the church. The Lord will / . . . keep you busy on weekends." Jordan's poem exposes the hazards of lesbian desire "within the circle" of prescribed/proscribed blackness.

Despite her privileging of heterosexuality and her use of homophobic epithets in her early poetry, Nikki Giovanni theorizes in 1970 with an ironic equanimity in "A Poem Because It Came As A Surprise To Me," appearing in her 1970 Broadside Press collection, *re creation*: "homosexuality /. . . . / is two people / of *similar* sex / DOING IT / that's all" (38, emphasis added). Giovanni's uppercase "DOING IT" is an emphatic dismissal of the Black Arts Movement commitments to heterosexual orthodoxy. She softens the enunciation of her shared epiphanic moment by choosing the vague descriptor, "similar," instead of "same," the preferred trope of the gay liberation movement.[4]

Consummate political poet, June Jordan, in "Metarhetoric," discards such weighty political subjects as "Homophobia/racism/self-definition/revolutionary struggle" for a "public discussion" of "our love." This "love" is quite insistent about calling its own name by asking for "the statistical dimensions / of

your mouth on my mouth / your breasts resting on my own"
(85).

Some braved the hazards of self-revelation. And later more
would brave them. Using as guide Alice Walker's singular essay,
"In Search of Our Mother's Gardens"(*Ms.* 1974), black lesbian
feminist critic Barbara Smith visited the gardens of black liter-
ary foremothers and ushered in the watershed era of black fem-
inist writing with her provocative 1977 essay, "Towards a Black
Feminist Criticism." Her assertions about reading black women's
writing generated unparalleled conversations that nearly thirty
years later still enrich black feminist thought.[5] Assertions such as
the following suggested that lesbianism was a broad intellectual
bed: "[Toni] Morrison's work poses both lesbian and feminist
questions about Black women's autonomy and their impact
upon each other's lives" (33).

Not content to keep herself busy on weekends with "the
Lord," Smith, on a panel, proposed the same theory at a Black
Writers Conference at Howard University in 1978.[6] June Jor-
dan was panel moderator, and copanelists with Smith were
Howard professor Acklyn Lynch and Black Arts poet Sonia
Sanchez. Smith thought herself on the solid ground of a
beloved black text when she made her claim that Morrison's
"*Sula* is an exceedingly lesbian novel in the emotions ex-
pressed," and she hastened to add that she did not mean to im-
pute lesbianism to Morrison and "not because the women are
'lovers,' but because [Sula and Nel] are the central figures, are
positively portrayed and have pivotal relationships with one
another."

A visceral collective groan resonated throughout the room
when Smith said the words "lesbian novel." We witnessed ex-
tremes of expressivity from a number of well-known figures of
the black cultural world—nationalists and non-nationalists—in
response to Smith's lesbian reading. Jordan held the stage, and
Smith held her position. The audience was finally subdued

enough for Stephen Henderson, Howard professor, scholar of black poetry, and conference organizer, to come onto the stage to close the session. Why was this racial confluence interrupted? Why was Smith's deployment of Black Arts Movement signifying, that is, critique of white cultural dominance and affirmation of black cultural traditions, refused? Because that deployment in the interest of a lesbian reading, albeit black, did not make for a happy nexus with the black literary public, hell-bent on having its writing be heterosexual.

Despite its exclusiveness, the uncompromising assertion of race identity politics practiced by Black Arts exponents served lesbian-feminist writers well—as it did much of the multicultural lesbian-feminist movement. The counter-historical narrative, the rejection of the "West," the reverence for same ("race" and/or "sex"), radical politics, radical rhetoric, claiming of the public, and the establishment of alternative cultural institutions and venues comprise the literacies black lesbian-feminists appropriated and reappropriated from the Black Arts Movement. Racist white feminists became objects of derision and less frequently sexist black men, as we see later.

Newspapers, journals, anthologies, presses, and bookstores were established in the 1970s. Jan Clausen, in her little-known literary history, *A Movement of Poets*, discusses the enabling power of these independent ventures, which corroborates Shange's discussion of the independent press and cultural venues available to her on the West Coast:

> By the mid-'70's, Diana Press and Daughters, Inc. had emerged as relatively powerful, well-organized lesbian controlled publishing efforts. Out & Out Books issued its first titles in 1975, among them *Amazon Poetry: An Anthology*, the largest collection of lesbian poetry then available, and the most comprehensive through the end of the decade. . . . Audre Lorde subsequently became poetry editor of *Chrysalis*,

begun in 1976—as was the more explicitly lesbian-focused *Sinister Wisdom*. *Azalea*, a magazine by and for Third World Lesbians, and *Conditions*, a magazine of women's writing with an emphasis on writing by lesbians, began publication in 1977. Throughout the mid-'70's, most feminist presses and periodicals published substantial amounts of poetry . . . [and were] extremely important to lesbian poets because of their role in the development of a specifically lesbian feminist literary culture and community. (17)

Women of color, including Afro-American women, became integral to this "lesbian-feminist literary culture and community," particularly in urban areas all over the country. Black lesbian feminists struggled with white lesbian feminists for reallocations of resources within their communities; and—along with other women of color—opened spaces within lesbian-feminist organizations for more diverse representation and participation. By the time black lesbian feminists became visible and active, the Black Power/Black Arts phase of the Afro-American freedom struggle had waned; and J. Edgar Hoover's counter-intelligence program had destroyed or disabled most revolutionary black nationalist organizations.

PARALLEL LONGINGS

By the time Pat Parker's *Movement In Black* was published by Diana Press in 1978, second-wave feminism had been shaking up patriarchy for almost fifteen years. *Movement in Black* is constructed as a black woman's emotional and political journey—a movement in black. Using the Black Arts tactic of speaking directly to one's enemy to make her argument against patriarchy, Parker's poem, "Exodus (To my husbands and lovers)," quietly refuses marriage, a cornerstone of compulsory heterosexuality: "i will serve you no more / in the name of wifely love / i'll not masturbate your pride / in the name of wifely loyalty"

(37). "Exodus" makes the analogy of so-called "wifely-love"/"wifely loyalty" to being a "desperate slave" caught within the "folds of cloth."

Using a technique of negative analogy, the irrepressible Nikki Giovanni in "Of Liberation," appropriates for her readers the stereotypes of lesbians and gays as weak and cowardly and tries to shame the indecisive subject, "black people," into organizing:

> Dykes of the world are united
> Faggots got their thing together
> (Everyone is organized)
> Black people these are facts
> Where's your power? (2)

Black Judge/Ment, the volume in which this poem appears, was published in 1968, a year before the Stonewall Rebellion in New York City,[7] which ushered in the Gay Liberation Movement. Perhaps we can credit Giovanni with predicting the new demands for homosexual rights. This poem is striking for its appropriation of what would become the reclaimed terms of lesbian and gay liberation to advance timeworn stereotypes of black people as unorganized, trifling, "3/5 of a man/100% whore" (2). Giovanni's poetry is a running critique of the unreadiness of black people for liberation, as we have seen. In 1972, Giovanni is crowned as "the princess of black poetry" by *Encore Magazine* editor and friend, Ida Lewis, who introduces Giovanni's second major press collection, *In My House*, in which she retreats from her Black Arts politics. The acerbic Michele Wallace makes deadly use of Lewis's accolade in her critique of Giovanni in *Black Macho and the Myth of the Superwoman*.

By 1973, Audre Lorde had allied her energies with interracial and progressive feminist groups. Like many political poets of the era, Lorde, also a teacher, a librarian, of Caribbean parentage but steady New Yorker, also lent her strong voice to many progressive, left, and international causes. Broadside Press's edition of Lorde's *From a Land Where Other People Live* (*A Land*) was nominated for a National Book Award in 1974, along with Norton's *Diving into the Wreck* by Adrienne Rich,[8] and Harcourt's *Revolutionary Petunias* by Alice Walker. All three books cross the restricted borders of race, sexuality, gender, and class. All three critique heterosexual, white, and male institutions, projects, and privilege. Lorde wrote most of her poems between 1969 and 1971 and signaled her rejection of the sexism and homophobia of black nationalism and the racism and classism of mainstream white feminism.

Also that same year, 1973, Lorde published *New York Headshop and Museum*. One of its poems, "Now," signifies on "Black Power" by rejecting the primacy of race: "Woman power / is / Black power / is / Human power / is" (*Undersong* 162). Implicitly refuting the black nationalist charge that feminism and blackness are binary opposites, Lorde makes them equivalents of being human. The succeeding five lines seem to describe a process of rebirth as a result of accepting the fluidity of these identities as well as their enabling powers. The title of the poem seems to admonish that there is no time like the present, that is, "Now," to accept the multiplicity of who one is. The poem rejects political narrowness and purity. Instead of castigation, as in "True Import," Lorde's speaker states her own readiness to take on the power of her multiple identities and asks: "Are you / Ready?"

NATIONALIST NOSTALGIA AND REVISIONIST MOTHERHOOD

The 1977 "A Black Feminist Statement," written by The Combahee River Collective, incorporated a manifesto that posited black feminism as radical praxis and ideology. It first appeared in Zillah Eisenstein's essay collection, *Capitalist Patriarchy and the Case for Socialist Feminism* in 1978. The statement opposes the "bourgeois feminist stance" of the National Black Feminist Organization, founded in 1973. The Combahee River Collective was its Boston chapter from 1974 to 1975. The statement has informed the theorizing of many progressive feminist groups. First, it makes clear that, though "a Black feminist presence has evolved in connection with the second wave" (Smith, ed. 265) black women, other women of color, and poor women have been involved with feminism since its nineteenth-century beginnings in the United States. By positing Black feminism's connection to historic "movements for Black Liberation," the statement eschews any kind of hierarchy of oppressions imposed upon black women and introduces the theory of the simultaneity of oppressions:

> We believe that sexual politics under patriarchy is as pervasive in Black women's lives as are the politics of class and race. We also often find it difficult to separate race from class from sex oppression because in our lives they are most often experienced simultaneously. We know that there is such a thing as racial-sexual oppression which is neither solely racial nor solely sexual, e.g., the history of rape of Black women by white men as a weapon of political repression. (267)

The Collective goes on to pronounce Black feminists' "solidarity with progressive Black men" and their unwillingness to "advocate the fractionalization that white women who are separatists demand." It critiques white feminists for "how little effort [they] have made to understand and combat their racism" (273). Finally, the statement holds its members and black feminists in general to "collective process and a non-hierarchical distribution of power within our own group and in our vision of a revolutionary society."

Yet, while racism, sexism, class oppression are emphasized throughout as the political "province" of black feminist struggle,

homophobia and heterosexism are not referenced at all, though
the writers refer to themselves as "feminists and lesbians" twice.
At one point the authors do admit that mounting a black femi-
nist political struggle is complicated by the fact that "we do not
have racial, sexual, *heterosexual*, or class privilege to rely upon"
(269, emphasis added). The subsuming of the lesbian by the
feminist identity functions in a way similar to Sanchez's elision
of any direct critique of black male behaviors discussed pre-
viously in the poem, "blk/rhetoric." Because the statement
accuses black men and black people of being "notoriously neg-
ative" toward and "threatened" by feminism (271), a strong
statement about the antigay and antilesbian attitudes of the
black community might risk driving more division between
black (lesbian) feminists and the black community. There is also
erasure of any but negative history of work with white feminists
on issues of gender and sexuality. While black feminists "must
struggle together with black men against racism" and "struggle
with black men about sexism" (267), "eliminating racism in the
white women's movement is by definition work for white
women to do" (273). A nostalgia for nationalism evinces itself in
the Statement, even though theoretically one would think that
because lesbian separatism was rejected so too would be any
form of black separatism.

Conventional motherhood came under heavy examination
during the seventies by both white and black feminists and les-
bian feminists. Yet, at the same time, poets like Adrienne Rich, a
mother of three and newly-become a lesbian, and Audre Lorde,
a self-defined black lesbian-feminist mother of two, were busy
reinventing and renegotiating motherhood. Rich, during this
time, had published a major feminist statement, *Of Woman Born*
in 1976. Lorde's references to children in her poems are
myriad—children are future, regeneration, and liberation from
the old paradigms. At the base of lesbian-feminist critiques of
motherhood is the struggle to separate sex from procreation.

Rich and Lorde, however, gave voice to the sensual and sexual feelings involved in mothering. Lorde, particularly, believed that women, feminists, lesbians should not give up mothering and constantly challenged women not to limit mothering to the biological and to "Speak proudly to your children / wherever you may find them" (*Chosen Poems* 43).

A BLACK UNICORN

The literacy gained from the Black Arts Movement became a large house of resistance to patriarchal culture—black and white. Audre Lorde's *The Black Unicorn* is an amazing statement of a black lesbian "cosmology and mythology" (Shariat, 1979), rooted in a mythic Dahomey, West Africa—where Lorde traces her own lineage of woman-centered consciousness. Black lesbian-feminism continued its expressivity throughout the 1980s, the era of Reaganism. Black lesbian pasts were recovered and invented by writers and critics like Jewelle Gomez, Gloria Hull, Ann Allen Shockley, and me—from within and without the accepted traditions of poetry and history. In "for muh dear," Carolyn Rodgers celebrates the black self's permeability to blackness, that is, "black lay backin and rootin" (*how i got ovah*1). Black Arts poetics "lay backin and rootin" in the culture of black lesbian feminists. Black lesbian feminist literacy of sexuality exposes the sexist and heterosexist (homophobic) commitments of the Black Arts Movement practitioners and simultaneously pays homage to the Black Arts Movement's revolutionary literacy.

My narrative of the workings of contemporary black women poets in the United States is not without its longings for symmetry. As Gwendolyn Brooks's 1968 elegy, "In the Mecca," is a meditation on the loss of lyric space in contemporary black poetry, Audre Lorde's 1978 *The Black Unicorn* is a meditation on the loss of political faith and a recuperation of a black matrilineal and lesbian diasporic literacy. Its Eshu-like narrator moves—

not unlike Brooks's narrator of "In the Mecca"—through time and space tolling the poems like sacrifices marking the terrain she traverses. *The Black Unicorn*, one of the most compelling books of the decade, posits a radically revised mythology for black lesbians, and indeed for all black women. "Unicorn," having the same metric resonance as "lesbian," functions as their (lesbians) sign.

The Black Unicorn is grounded in an Afrocentric pastiche of signifiers. It most markedly departs from Shange, Walker, Brooks and black diasporic literary traditions in that it constructs a black lesbian feminist mythopoetic space that puts black women at the center. In Lorde's cosmology, black women are going to have to come to terms with their Amazon (women-loving-women and warrior) past, and learn—as she says in her article, "I Am Your Sister"—to use their power to organize "across sexualities" (*A Burst of Light* 19–27). The perimeter of *The Black Unicorn* is less proscribed than those of *for colored girls* and the Black Arts Movement, but it is also less communal and more fragmented. The "I" of these poems claims West Africa and key figures of its pantheon of Orishas (deities) as her kin: Eshu, Seboulisa, Mawulisa. Yet, as other critics have stated, Africa is not Lorde's only "home." She must claim two others—the Caribbean, the homeland of her parents, and the United States, her place of birth and survival. Like her literary sisters, Paule Marshall in *Chosen Place, Timeless People* and *Praisesong for the Widow*, and Toni Morrison in *Tar Baby*, Lorde's poems in *The Black Unicorn* traverse the Black Atlantic Diaspora (Chinasole 392). Lorde's *Zami* and *Our Dead Behind Us* further exemplify this Black Atlantic Diaspora. In fact, black feminist critics have suggested that *Zami* and *The Black Unicorn* be read side-by-side for fuller comprehension of each (Chinasole); and that the 1986 *Our Dead Behind Us* is a continuation of the statements and propositions Lorde set forth in *The Black Unicorn* (Hull 153). However, I construct *The Black Unicorn* as a signifying black lesbian feminist text, at the edge of the repressive 1970s: gesturing back/recovering a matriarchal/matrilineal/lesbian Africa, synthesizing those lessons in an Afro-American place and consciousness, and projecting a cautionary feminist poetics into the approaching era of Reagan, Meese, Bush, Idi Amin, and AIDS. I wish to examine Lorde's poetics of lamentation and recuperation in select poems from *The Black Unicorn*. She offers exquisite portraits of love/intimacy as a series of "small deaths" (64). Wherever she is the terrain is dangerous or brutal, including most definitely and defiantly the terrain of human relationships. The West, specifically the United States, is a place of death as Lorde had learned well from the Black Arts Movement.

An antiqued photograph of a West African headdress, set off against a background of magenta, with the book's title, genre, and author announcing themselves in large point white and black letters to the left, constitutes the cover art of *The Black Unicorn*. For the sake of paradox and marketability the title appears in white letters. The genre, "poems," in understated lowercase black letters a point size smaller than the title and directly underneath makes itself flush with the title. The author's name directly underneath "poems" in title-case black letters and flush beckons the reader. The headdress is horned resembling the shape of the unicorn, that fabled horselike creature with a horn in the middle of its head, usually depicted as white. The headdress represents both propitiation and fecundity. Certainly, there is nothing in the present that can propitiate this poet or her muse. But the possibility of harvest always leavens her despair.

Lorde's dedication to her parents Linda and Frederick reprises the West African tradition of honoring one's ancestors, perhaps propitiating them. "The Face Has Many Seasons," Lorde's inscription to the collection, signifies her refusal to give into binaries and false dichotomies. The collection is comprised of sixty-eight poems in four parts.

The poems of part 1 pay homage to West African spirituality, with their constant references to its female deities, for example, Seboulisa, Mawulisa, Yemanya. The collection opens with the title poem, "The Black Unicorn." In this spare sixteen-line narrative, the speaker uses only copulas to declare her present state—"greedy .... impatient .... restless .... unrelenting .... not free" (3). There are muted references to an horrific past, perhaps the Atlantic slave trade, perhaps other kinds of coerced relations. This section enunciates Lorde's poetics. In the following lines the person shifts from third- to first-person possessive, as if the speaker were collapsing any distinction between self and the black unicorn: "The black unicorn was . . . taken / through a cold country / where mist painted mockeries / of *my* fury (3). Immediately at the next line, the speaker shifts back to third-person voice and distances herself from the subject again: "It is not on her lap where the horn rests / but deep in her moonpit / growing."

"Moonpit" is a Lordean reference to the vulva; and "the horn," seemingly phallic as befitting Eshu, signals permeability, essence, fecundity. Eshu is an androgynous figure, who at times is depicted with an erect penis. However, Eshu's female principle will be honored here. Akasha (Gloria) Hull, in "Living on the Line," her superb article on *Our Dead Behind Us*, sees Lorde's constant rhetorical and prosodic movement along borders, edges, lines, intersections, crossroads as her unwillingness to become comfortable with connection for fear that something crucial "is being glossed over" (155). Lorde refuses the circle. So, too, the black unicorn, who, finally, is "restless," "unrelenting," and "not free."

The female principle is invoked more directly in "A Woman Speaks," which follows "The Black Unicorn." In this poem, Lorde continues to theorize on the imperatives of duality, synthesis, and loss:

Moon-marked and touched by sun . . . .
I do not dwell
within my birth nor my divinities
who am ageless and half-grown
and still seeking
my sisters. (4)

The last line of "A Woman Speaks" connects with the last line of "The Black Unicorn" as each negates that which neither claims to be: "I am / woman / and not white" (5). The speaker is both confessional and admonitory and carries tremendous authority. (Sometimes she throws her weight around.)

"From the House of Yemanja," "Coniagui Women," "Dahomey," "125th Street and Abomey," "The Women of the Dan Dance with Swords in their Hands To Mark the Time When They were Warriors," "Sahara," the last six poems of "Part I," are companion pieces and will be discussed as a narrative of the poet's reclamation of her matrilineal African roots. Mothers are perpetual signs of creativity and destruction in Lorde's work. They are often angry, withholding, and cruel.

Yemanja of the long breasts from whom rivers are said to flow, goddess of oceans, sign of fecundity, mother of all the orishas is the speaker's stern mother also: "My mother had two faces and a frying pot" (6). Typically, Lorde blurs distinctions between spiritual and biological progenitors. This is a poem of longing for the terrible legacies of mothers, a blending of the spiritual and domestic, and an allusion to the "two-headed doctor" in conjure (vodun) practices. In stuttering pronouncements, the speaker cries for Yemanja: "Mother I need / mother I need / mother I need your blackness now."

In "Coniagui Women" Lorde tells a different creation story of children "who have eight days to choose their mothers" (8) and mocks the patriarchal Old Testament "Genesis" and other

patriarchal myths by rejecting the primacy of men. The mythol-
ogized longing of sons for their mothers' bed is replayed in the
triple refrain of "'Let us sleep in your bed' they whisper."
Though they have no speech among the Coniagui women, the
sons attempt to seduce their mothers' power of language. The
triple refrain recalls the lines from "Yemanja" quoted above.
Both appeals foreground mothers as an essential creative and
willful force whose rejection of their sons not only causes the
sons to become men but also reverses other mythologies of eros
between mothers and sons.

In "Dahomey," the poet's (bio)mythographic home and an-
other West African construct and icon,[9] the authoritative
speaker recovers a language of resistance: "Bearing two drums
on my head I speak / whatever language is needed / to sharpen
the knives of my tongue . . . . / I am a woman whether or not /
you are against me" (11). Dahomey, an ancient West African
kingdom, home of the mythic Amazons, is a place of discovery.
"Seboulisa," "goddess of Abomey," is another figure of regenera-
tion/recuperation. The 1970s was a period of excavation of and
reflection upon histories. Although Abomey is women's space,
"Brothers and nephews" are allowed in the courtyard, even as
they foretell their own destructiveness in the "bright tapestries"
they are stitching (10).

Following "Dahomey" is "125th Street and Abomey," in
which the poet continues to connect the sources of her creativ-
ity as she blurs these two creative sites of blackness. Seboulisa is
again invoked—this time in Harlem—where the poet pays
homage to her African sources. As in many poems of part 1,
Lorde prays for the power to speak, write, and translate as the
ancient "warrior sisters" (12) protected the "queendom" of Se-
boulisa. The poet's "strength of tongue" becomes a weapon
against the "cold season," perhaps both a reference to the "sor-
row and loss" of the post–Black Power era and a tribute to the
tongue as the weapon that survived the Middle Passage. How-

ever, finally the "severed daughter" prays to her "mother god-
dess," Seboulisa for reunion and recognition.

In "The Women of Dan Dance With Swords In Their Hands
To Mark The Time When They Were Warriors" the poet rejects
Western mythologies, primarily Greco-Judaeo-Roman concepts
of divinity. She locates herself in Dahomey again; "Dan" is the
ancient name for this ancient site of the Amazons, from whom
Lorde draws her warrior legacy. Not "a secret warrior," she re-
jects the mask of submissiveness and self-hatred "slicing my
throat to ribbons / of service with a smile" (14). The supplica-
tion is prophetic and full of sexual double entendre:

> I come as a woman
> dark and open . . . .
> I come like a woman
> who I am
> spreading out through nights
> laughter and promise . . . . (15)

The terrain of part 2 is the United States. The voices here
are rich with cautionary tales. Mother-daughter connections are
longed for and reconstituted in part 1, not so in part 2. Begin-
ning with the elegiac "Harriet," the poems call on the African
"sisters" in the New World to deal with their atonement. Har-
riet is a muse of sorts. She stands for the women women love
and forsake for the purpose of "keeping our distance." Lorde's
"we were / nappy girls quick as cuttlefish" evokes Nel's excla-
mation upon Sula's death in Toni Morrison's *Sula*: "We was girls
together." The loss of that intimacy is lamented here. There are
muted references to the historic as well as the mythic past; and
the struggle for language and literacy is characterized by three
repetitions of the literal act: "tyring to speak trying to speak /
trying to speak" (21). No caesura between the first two utter-
ances and a line break at the third, again create a stuttering ef-
fect or the effect of Shange's/Fanon's "combat breath."

"Harriet" is a poem of black women's personal and historic failure to connect with one another since being "broken apart" from the mythological and historic mothers, the "warrior queens," the slave mothers, the mothers who, like Morrison's Sethe, must repress their love for their daughters because of the anticipated loss: "Harriet Harriet / what name shall we call our selves now / our mother is gone?" The repetition of Harriet's name once again indicates the speaker's failure to locate an un-perverted language, a "name" in the absence of the mother.

In *The Terrible Stories* (1997), Lucille Clifton reveals in poems her experience of incest committed upon her by her father. Upon that revelation, one can understand how the incest expe-rience allows her to animate the voices of slaves in her earlier work *Good Times* and *Generations*; for example, the slave woman's voice in the poem "If he ask you was I laughing" (*Good Woman* 34). Child sexual abuse, like slavery, is a coerced relationship. Neither the enslaved person nor the sexually-abused child chooses it. The site of Lorde's terrible story, "Chain," is contemporary New York City. In an untypically long poem, Lorde structures in two parts a woeful tale-within-in-a-tale of incest committed by a father upon his two daugh-ters and their subsequent pregnancies. The poem opens in a seemingly enclosed space, like a courtroom perhaps, where the speaker announces "the skeleton children advancing against us"—the parents, juries, caseworkers, and poets, whose values have not protected the children from violations that can be construed as "love." What is this "love," the poem asks.

One of Lorde's great concerns is intergenerational responsi-bility and accountability—another example of her looking-back-looking-forward strategy or what AnaLouise Keating calls her "threshold politics" (2). Damage done to daughters is also her great concern, as we have seen in her 1972 poem, "To My Daughter the Junkie on a Train" from *New York Headshop and Museum* (*Undersong* 144). In part "II" of "Chain," the site shifts to the speaker's front porch "covered with bodies / of young girls" (23). The speaker imagines the two teenage sisters with babies by their father, standing in her doorway, and becomes a figure of their mother. In two complicated and extensive stanzas, the speaker imagines that she allows both "daughters" to rehearse their anger at their "mother's" inability to name the relationship that has coerced each daughter to become her father's lover. "Chain" is a poem that mourns more than the physical deaths children die—namely, the death of dreams, the death of feeling protected from forces larger than oneself. "Winter has come and the children are dying" (23). Indeed.

"Sequelae" is a paradoxical and parodic elegy, distinguished by deep images of burning and exquisitely visceral, highly dramatic language. Not quite a sequel to "Chain," it mourns a history of morbid affections—love relationships. Unlike conventional elegies, it does not praise the persons/lovers who are lost, nor does it offer consolation. The emotional detritus of memories is lamented here: "my pathways are strewn with old discontents / outgrown defenses still sturdy as firebrick" (26).

Lorde splices her tight metaphors with quotidian images like "cornflakes" and "measles." Above all "Sequelae" is emblematic of Lorde's uses of the lyric to expose the rankness—the lover's and her beloved's—in the dissolution of the relationship. In Lorde "hate" and "love" stand in for one another: "hating you for being / black and not woman / hating you for being white / and not me" (25).

She carries forward the questions raised in "Chain" about the conditions of love in intimate relations, that is, vulnerability, instability, and surrender. The very intriguing passage above alludes to her race and gender concerns and the dangers and seductions of false oppositions and fears of contamination. One must wear one's contradictions and contaminations in the same way one must live with ghosts (25). Later race appears again in the guise of "black and white faces / saying no over and over"

(26), restricting as parents. In being transported from love to the death of love, the speaker is transported to another place, typical of an elegy. But in this postmodern reversal, in this "moment of time / where the space ships land," there is no consolation nor surcease from lament.

She recuperates the black woman warrior in the figure of contemporary black revolutionary Assata Shakur.[10] Once again, Lorde chooses a subject who is emblematic of the era. Shakur was, after Angela Davis, the most publicized black woman revolutionary to be captured, and for Lorde is a signifier of the loss of revolution. Speaking is a crucial trope of liberation, especially for women and a concern that Lorde raises again and again in her prose as well as her poetry. The imprisoned Shakur, who has let go of the "vanities of silence" (28), signifies also the loss of speech. In Shakur, Lorde sees other "sisters / who have not yet spoken" and in dreaming of Shakur's freedom dreams of victory for "all dark women" who speak and act against "our enemies." Lorde speaks to her constant concern that sisters, "who forego silence," too often turn the rage of their speech against "ourselves in each other." Addressing and allying with Shakur as "my sister warrior," she commends her to the spirits of two other sister warriors, that is, to "Joan of Arc and Yaa Asantewaa," who "embrace/at the back of your cell," allowing her mythopoetic strategy to recuperate other women warriors.

What is beyond the death of children and other heroes, of movements, of revolutions, of love? Survivors. "A Litany for Survival" subverts the conventional public prayer. Not to some vague deity go its petitions, but to the survivors, "those . . . who live at the shoreline / standing upon the constant edges of decision / crucial and alone," looking back and looking forward (31). The poem makes use of enjambment and long lineation in its identification of those included in this call. The poet/priest calls for a collectivity, the "us" and the "we," to cross the line between survival and "[the] now that can breed / futures," a "new *now*," as Houston Baker asserts about the space and time black women writers are always making. Neither exclusive race nor exclusive gender nor exclusive sexuality defines this collectivity, consonant with Lorde's communal visions. Anyone "who cannot indulge / the passing dreams of choice" may answer this call, may speak this "litany," very different from Baraka's "SOS"—"calling all black people to come on in." As a black lesbian feminist sister outsider, Lorde spent her life speaking to outsiders and "outlaws," those of us at those edges. As an African-descent lesbian, she "crosses and recrosses" the lines between outsider and outlaw. The duality of "crucial and alone" once again demonstrates Hull's insights about lines and intersections in Lorde's poetry. "Crucial" suggests decisiveness while evoking the form of a cross, the notion of crossroads, ambivalence, and a kind of contrary indecisiveness—both/and. These crossroads presented themselves throughout the seventies as political movements waxed and waned. Particularly, after the demise of the Black Power Movement by 1975, reassessment and reevaluation of positions, lines, and energies, were in high evidence in the lives and writings of activist women and men—both of color and white. Questions of how to recuperate and how to move on, how to continue to resist and to remain subversive without discarding strategies of reclamation, were asked silently and loud. "Alone" is Lorde's trope for courage here.

Fear, "this weapon . . . this illusion," is the subject of the poem's second stanza. The speaker also places herself among "those of us / who were imprinted with fear / like a faint line in the center of our foreheads" (31). Courage is neither a given nor a constant. Nor is fear. The speaker instructs the collectivity that silence has not protected "us" nor has fear prevented "our" survival. Matter of factly, she reminds us that we have triumphed despite historic intentions of the "heavy-footed" to destroy us: "We were never meant to survive."

Lorde counsels against the Western trap of false dichotomies in much of her writing. She illuminates the fear of the oppressed to hope and to trust in the most basic satisfactions, to see beyond the shoreline. Breaking the silence is a major trope of resistance for Lorde in her writing and in her life. The consequences of speaking can be no worse than those of silence in the face of our enemies. She theorizes here in her poetry for the first time that as fear coexists with silence then so it coexists with speaking:

> when we speak we are afraid
> our words will not be heard
> nor welcomed
> but when we are silent
> we are still afraid. (32)

With the authority of mothers, she makes us believe that it is "better to speak" *with* our fear than be silent with it. Loss may be the consequence of either strategy. Recuperating histories of past atrocities further serves to break silences. When read publicly this poem galvanized diverse women's audiences. The repetitions, refrains, and straight-forward language allow access to the lesson. The priestly function of the speaker is familiar and comforting. Its appeal to experience—the experience of being alone, being afraid, being unable to speak or write or say, letting silence betray self or someone else—makes possible a vision beyond survival.

Lorde was among a community of pioneers who broke the silence by writing about lesbian sexuality and the erotic. Her earliest lyrics subverted conventions with their refusals to identify the gender of the speaker, to perform heterosexuality (or homosexuality for that matter), and to make men the object of desire. In "Anniversary," a 1953 poem of loss, which was published in her first book, *First Cities* (1968), she addresses the beloved who is dead, perhaps by suicide. The metaphors, "bride" and "sister," signify the gender of the beloved (*Collected Poems* 209). Wherever she found herself, she used poetry to plumb the emotional geography and genealogy of love between women. Many of the love poems in *The Black Unicorn* imagine distant worlds, perhaps a future of desolation or a remove to primordial terrains, high in the mountains, by rivers, in caves, or in gardens, rarely in urban spaces. The lover is always wary of the relationship, its precariousness; the beloved is often distant, withholding. Love occurs in the midst of danger. Neither love's nor the lover's nor the beloved's survival is a foregone conclusion.

After a series of highly suggestive images and highly explicit sexual references in the poem "Meet," the lover compares their love to kinships that have survived many hostile incursions: "now you are my child and my mother / we have always been sisters in pain" (34). The final stanza is mystifying, hyperbolic, and dramatic. The lover says, "we have mated we have cubbed," as if saying they, like the lion, have satisfied nature. There is an earlier reference to the beloved "licking her sons" (33). Lorde often blurs distinctions between human sexuality/maternity and that of animals. Now, "in the innermost rooms of moment" (34), they have a brief time for "exchanging" their women's blood like ancient warriors who are preparing for battle. We can make Lorde's metaphors applicable to the fatalism, paranoia, and flight from "home" which characterized the 1970s.

"Walking Our Boundaries" uses the metaphorical resonances of the natural world as vehicle for understanding the emotional turmoil of love relationships, that is, "war." The lines, "We rise from war / to walk across the earth / around our house," place the reader formidably in "last year's garden," where the speaker/lover and the beloved survey the ravages of winter. This, in turn, causes her also to reflect upon "all our pain" (38).

However, the "bracken," the "one tough okra pod," the "parody of fruit," which survived winter like their relationship, make the speaker "glad to be alive and still / with" her beloved.

"Walking Our Boundaries" is another example of Keating's notion of Lorde's "threshold" positionality as the speaker looks back at the damage "last winter's storm" wrought upon "our ancient apple tree," and ahead to "next week [when] we will spade up another plot / for this spring's seeding" (39). This is a weighty poem, self-consciously so with its well-worked enjambment and resistant to any euphoric or pastoral sense of spring. Like much of this collection, "Walking" is attentive to the precariousness and fragility of life—all life and all lives—and tightly pairs the emotional world and the natural world, the garden and the relationship, their survival of winter/war, their desire for spring/intimacy. Almost self-correcting, the speaker rejects the symbolism of the "ancient apple tree" to hold (or reconnect with) the "substance," the body and surrenders to her longing: "my shoulders are dead leaves/ waiting to be burned / to life."

"Burned" signifies the survival of the erotic, but "the sun is watery warm." Continuing to resist symbols, the speaker is aware of the limitations of both figurative and literal readings. Love relationships do not always fit the context in which they exist: "our voices / seem too loud for this small yard / too tentative for women / so in love / the siding has come loose in spots" (39). Who they are is too large to be contained by a yard, siding, or a metaphor. Yet, they have adapted to the "place" where their "joint decisions" are made as they have adapted to the "place" of their intimacy. Nothing is inevitable, and everything is precarious, though certain rituals prevail.

"In Margaret's Garden" mourns a woman's failure to know herself beyond the definitions of others. Literacy of the self is as critical for Lorde as it is for Shange. She likens its lack to a "mouth . . . smiling / off-center / in total confusion" (47). Intimacy for Lorde means fear, shame, hatred, risk, and risk of self-revelation—but going there anyway. A garden is a place of life, death, survival, and potential, as she demonstrates in "Walking Our Boundaries." Margaret's refusal to "confront her own pain" stunts her garden's potential.

Lorde like Shange is willing to expose the dirty secrets of each of her communities—the black, the lesbian, the feminist. She has spoken in lecture, poem, and essay on the problems of self-hatred, intraracial hatred, and misogyny and homophobia in the black community. Her caustic 1966 poem "Family Resemblance," might be an early meditation on self-hatred: "My sister has my hair my mouth / my eyes / and I presume her trustless" (*Undersong* 41). The "family resemblance" is a larger reference than the biological family. In "Eye to Eye: Black Women, Hatred, and Anger," her 1983 essay from *Essence* (Oct., 14, no. 6) and reprinted in an abbreviated form in *Sister Outsider: Essays and Speeches*, asks rhetorically of a self, generalized to the community of black women: "Why do I judge her [another black woman] in a more critical light than any other, becoming enraged when she does not measure up?" (145).

The narrator moves into another sphere in which judgment is rife, that of political movements. "A Song For Many Movements" warns of the toll the various struggles have taken on their warriors, "caught between ghosts of whiteness / and the real water" (52). It also seems a critique of the religiouslike zeal, appeals to false unity, and the common grief that generate as well as destroy movements: "none of us wanted to leave / our bones / on the way to salvation." The "broken down gods" in the second stanza are the political ideologies that once fueled movements but now survive "in the crevasses and mudpots of every beleaguered city," desolate with too many bodies "to bury or burn." I am mystified by the way Lorde uses "silence" in this poem.

> and our uses have become
> more important than our silence
> after the fall
> . . . . and our labor
> has become more important
> than our silence.
>
> Our labor has become
> more important
> than our silence.

More important to whom? I am not convinced she is exhorting "us" to speak, as she does in the "Transformation of Silence into Language and Action" in *The Cancer Journals*; there she enunciates the privileges and particularly the dangers of silence. For Lorde, silence is never strategic; it portends deadly fear and collusion, which prevent speaking, which prevent concerted political action, which keep people in their various "closets," like prosthesis conceals the fact of a woman's mastectomy/ies. It is better to speak, she says, and be afraid than to remain silent and still be afraid. She sees many h[H]olocausts, many "ovens and gallows" (52). Silence did not prevent them. However, above, her meaning seems less stable. She repeats the lines three times with slight but significant alteration. Our instrumentality, "uses" and "labor," to political movements, "broken down gods," supercedes any claims we may have on our own lives, that is, on our "silence" (or privacy.)

Lorde moves from silence to the public in "Outside," the opening poem of part 3. The speaker positions herself "in the center of a harsh and spectrummed city," looking back at the legacies of her mother and father and looking ahead to forging her own: "they have both marked me / with their blind and terrible love / and I am lustful now for my own name" (62) The poem ends with a celebration of many parts of the self or the "my selves" without the fracturing and splitting off that occurs when human differences are rejected and erased.

"The Same Death Over and Over / Or / Lullabies Are For Children" is one of a series of poems in this volume which commemorates the police shooting death of ten-year-old Clifford Glover in New York City in 1976. The speaker expresses her rage at the death of this black child in a "predawn city / where it is open season on black children." As I have said previously, children, for Lorde, as for many black women writers, are futurity and possibility and their murders are the "unmaking" of us all" (64).

She reprises her concern for the deaths of black children in a poem "for Clifford," entitled "A Woman/Dirge For Wasted Children." This lament for Clifford, sacrificed on the altar of race hatred, is particular; it is a "Woman/Dirge." The first two words of the title split and cleave the meaning of the poem's address. The assertion (of gender) claims space for women in the production of this ancient form for singing over the dead. The slash also tells us that a woman speaks (sings) for "wasted children" and that this poem is their "dirge." True to its tradition, this dirge does not console. In fact, the speaker is intensely focused on the agency of her own grief. The "I" is emphatic and unitary, particularizing the grief and marking it as "Woman's." The speaker derives great power from her "benediction of fury," the burning empathy with the dead black boy, shot in the back by a white policeman who thought he saw a gun in the child's hand.

Brought on by the profanation of child murder, the speaker's searing and highly imagistic language signifies her rage. Her invocation of the "thunder goddess," probably MawuLisa, Dahomean "sky god-goddess" principle, supplants Shango, the Yoruba god of thunder popularized during the Black Arts Movement, and emboldens her Woman's stance. No sacrifice can reverse the deed, therefore "one drop of [her] blood" is expiation/libation enough. This dirge is not a revision of African-American funerary ritual, in which consolation of mourners is central, the laying on of hands. It eschews visions of Jordan for the stark image of urban terrain.

She moves from the imaginary of ritual to the mundane evil of a late twentieth-century antiabortionist who has had himself "appointed/legal guardian of fetuses." She counters this absurd irony with her own egocentric vision of paradox and hyperbole: "Centuries of wasted children / warred and whored and slaughtered / anoint me guardian / for life" (66). The assonance and internal rhyme of the second line emphasize the progressive horror of this history as it gives her the agency to give the history voice. Back again in the "early light," in the final section, still refusing consolation, the speaker is, as usual in Lorde's poems, seeing out, envisioning a future of wiping up the aborted lives of black children.

Most of the remaining poems of "Section III" are homoerotic lyrics, as exquisite as any love lyrics in English. Rich in ambiguity, imagery, conceit, and pathos, Lorde's lyrics in *The Black Unicorn* reveal the uncertainty of love between women "in this misty place" (70). Assuming the conventional first person stance, with its unitary "I" and deploying the rhetoric of indirection, Lorde revises the lyric and writes lesbians into its tradition. She genders neither the lover nor the beloved, except in the poem, "Woman," in which the title serves as the speaker's address. Lorde's strategy of indirection is not a gesture of passing or concealing but rather a play on the reader's assumption that her woman-identification is always-already performed in her love poetry.

Marcellus Blount remarks at length on nineteenth-century, Harlem Renaissance, and post-Renaissance uses of lyric by black poets as a place to resist rigid gender and sex role prescriptions, to speak the self in the other (Boone and Cadden, eds. 225–239). Lorde uses her lyric "'I/eye'" (236) to witness the experience of sex/love between women in a racist, hetero-sexist, and misogynist culture that kills children. No lower case "i" for this poet. Adrienne Rich had already lyricized lesbian love in her 1970s chapbook, *Twenty-One Love Poems*, which was later included in her stunning 1978 *The Dream of a Common Language*; and Marilyn Hacker would do so again in 1986 in her book-length sonnet sequence, *Love, Death, and the Changing of the Seasons*.

Self-knowledge and self-love are critical to Lorde's vision of change. Critically and artistically she holds herself and other poets/women accountable. In "Uses of the Erotic as Power," she claims the erotic is the deepest part of self-knowledge, enabling joy and the ability to share joy (*Sister Outsider* 56). In "Poetry Is Not A Luxury," she historicizes women's rejection of "the euro-pean mode" for the "hidden sources of our power" (37). In "The Uses of Anger: Women Responding to Racism," Lorde constructs anger, like the erotic. It must be acknowledged and applied. She begs the question of white women's resistance to black women's anger as an inability to confront their own anger and therefore to know themselves: "My response to racism is anger . . . . Once I did it in silence, afraid of the weight. My fear of anger taught me nothing. Your fear of that anger will teach you nothing, also" (124). She warns white women that respond-ing to racism is responding to (black women's) anger: "The anger of exclusion, of unquestioned privilege, of racial distor-tions, of silence, ill-use, stereotyping, defensiveness, misnaming, betrayal, and co-optation."

The ability to know oneself, to share joy, to express anger, to confront the other's anger are essential literacies in intimate relationships. Rarely addressing the complexity of intimacy in her essays, Lorde uses poetry to theorize about it. Knowledge of self enables the embrace of difference and the struggle for inti-macy. The failure of love relationships in much of her poetry re-flects the lover's or the beloved's failure to know the self.

"Parting" is a deft love lyric with an intense, compressed narrative. The beloved, trapped in her self-destruction, necessitates the lover's parting. Evoking Dunbar's metaphor in his 1896 lyric "Sympathy" of the black poet as a caged bird, Lorde's opening line alliterates—"belligerent and beautiful"—releasing the incisive image of a "trapped ibis" (68). As she turns away from the beloved and her deficient self-love, the lover juxtaposes a final symbolic vision of the self-destructiveness with her own self-wounding attempts at consolation, "licking my heart / for moisture / cactus-tongued."

"Timepiece" is more laudatory of love. Its opening section is one long Shange-like stanza of enjambment and atavistic, exotic, mythic references, as the two lovers sail "upstream for water / Elegba's clay pot whistling" upon the head of the beloved. Often in Lorde's lyrics, the lovers move between primordial and present time, uneasy in both. In the "Glossary of African Terms Used in the Poems" provided by Lorde at the end of the volume, we learn that Es[h]u/Elegba, West African god of the unpredictable who has no priests and whose part in rituals is often acted by a woman with an "attached phallus" (19), is invoked again in the image of the "priestess," on whose ground the lovers "tell the course / of each other's tongue / with stones." The tongue is a metonym for speaking love and for making it. Rarely explicit about sex, Lorde's metphor is unabashedly transparent and resonant:

> in the place where the priestess
> hurtled out palm-nuts
> from enchanted fingers
> and stones mix
> the colors of rainbows
> flashing
> you came like a wheaten song. (69)

"Fog Report" returns us to the problematic tropes of desire, as the lover speaks of her inability to be individuated from the beloved, "I am too close to you to be useful" (70). Lack of clarity has structured this relationship, thus, the lover occupies a "misty place" where this lyric functions as a "Fog Report." Insufficiency manipulates desire, "hunger finds us seeking direction." This poem also advances Lorde's theory that one loathes in others what one loathes in oneself; and one loves in others what one cannot love in oneself: "it is easier for me / to move / against myself in you / than to solve my own equations" (70).

Neither the lover nor the beloved seems equipped with self-knowledge. The graphic representation of the "shape" of the beloved's teeth "written into" the lover's "palm" makes an emphatic assertion of the lover's mental engrossment and haunted existence. The conceit of obsession is made more powerful by the paradoxical, sensual/sexual, and strangely forensic imagery: "when I am fingerprinted / the taste of your thighs / shows up / outlined in the ink."

In the last stanza, the lover engages in a violent fantasy of transforming the beloved "into my own forgotten image" by reconstructing her "orifices"—a telling fantasy. Presumably once "reconstructed," the fog will lift, and the beloved will be "tethered like a goat / in my heart's yard," certainly not a wide perimeter. As in "Parting," the visceral heart is referenced. In "Fog Report," it is a metaphor of confinement; in "Parting" the heart is a place of unattained consolation.

In "Recreation," which signifies on the title of Nikki Giovanni's 1970 book of poems, *re creation*, the lover explores anew the issue of regeneration, so important to the Black Arts poets and to the nascent, interracial lesbian feminist poetry writing community of which Lorde became a participant and arbiter. With Lorde's supple poetics, the notion regeneration takes on particular and different meanings for lesbians. The poem opens with the pun of "Coming together." It opposes narcissism and repression by positing mutuality between the lovers, who find it "easier to work after our bodies / meet" (81). Their "work" is writing, and they discover that "paper and pen" are not the only means through which "the poem" is created. The lover recounts how she and her beloved re-create one another in the act of sex. Lorde calls for women to use the erotic to rewrite, re-invent, regenerate women's dynamic/creative powers: "You create me against your thighs / hilly with images" (81).

In "Ghost," Lorde explores the ghost of memory as the lover struggles to mourn a past relationship in which neither the lover nor the beloved could "bear" or "question" the other's "dreams." In fact, the lover rehearses a past act of the beloved's betrayal: "crying out in your sleep / to another woman / come play in the snow love" (85). Once again the act of writing is referenced, but here instead of a means of re-creation, writing threatens to restore her memory of the "season of cold" that was their relationship. The oppositional sensations evoked by the rather cornball "snowflakes of love melting into ice" underscores the lover's testimonial: "Now this poem / makes those mornings real again" (85). In an odd aside, someone named "Bernice," possibly a more recent former lover, is inserted into the present of the poem and momentarily distracts the lover and us from the more remote memories of pain:

"Artisan" reveals an artful lover who delights in her exuberant lyric, full of paradoxes and ambiguous caesuras, and the discovery of the other's vulva. In fact, the first stanza is a tribute to that vulva. Light and dark are never binary opposites in Lorde. Here they function as fields of vision. The first paradoxical image of "workshops without light" finds the lovers together making incomplete artifacts of "birds that do not sing" and "kites that shine / but cannot fly." They are "we," and not split into I/lover and you/beloved until the "light falls / in the throat /of delicate working fire," causing the lover to distance herself to enjoy an exquisite vision of the beloved's vulva.

The image of "a case of tortoise shell / hung / in the mouth of darkness" creates a compelling image of the labia as a decorative object, which the mottled tortoise shell sometimes becomes. Under the "carapace," suggestive of labia, the lover moves to find, in the teasing assonance, the "sweet meat" beneath. The emphatic and extended caesura after "beneath" functions metrically and performatively, much as it did in Donne's love lyrics, to give indeterminate discursive space to sex.

The lover's ironic recognition of self in the act of lovemaking causes her to realize what she had not known: "I did not recognize / the shape / of my own name." The hard and again extended caesura after "name," functions similarly as before, as a discursive space of action, change, transformation. In that space the split between subject and object dissolves into the conciliatory metaphor of: "Our bed spread / is a midnight flower." "Coming / all the way down to the floor," the lover intent upon seeing her beloved's vulva, splits off again to delight in "your craft." The lover seems as interested in spectatorship as self-knowledge. One wonders, given this distancing, whether the lover ever learns the shape of her own name.

"The Old Days," a somber address, opens Part 4, the final section, and seems to correct the nostalgia of Part 3's closing poem "Bicentennial Poem #21, 100,000." Lorde appropriates an even more hackneyed popular culture trope than the 1976 U.S. bicentennial: "the good old days," abbreviates it to "the old days," exposing the dangers and tragedies of living as a lesbian in the post-McCarthy fifties. News of a lover's death probably occasions the poem. "The old days" is an allusion to the pre-Stonewall confined social spaces and the requisite hostile social climate for homosexual lovers. Full of vague and cherished memories for some, "the old days" always signifies some other people's precise hell, in this case that of lesbians. The speaker's memory of the old days is that of a hard darkness whose only light is:

the harsh searing eye
of unblinking madwomen and men

calling our star a zoo
and I have no bride to recall
only many women who whisper
I was always a virgin
because I never remained. (93)

Because of the elision of "mad" and "women," one might read it as only they, and not the "men" as well, who are are "unblinking" and "mad." Perhaps the women like the speaker are driven to the edges because of the "men calling our star a zoo." But perhaps, it is merely a reference to the homophobia of the mental health profession of "the old days," which catalogued "homosexuality" as disease. The "many women who whisper" are those who remained caught in the world of "twilight lovers." The speaker passed out of that world, therefore, remaining uninitiated or "a virgin." The reference to matrimony is a parodic gesture enabling the speaker to expose both homosexuals' desire to conform as well as the irony of appropriating heterosexual rituals. The speaker's memory of "the old days" of proscribed craziness and self-hatred causes her to remember what she had forgotten: the name of a dead lover remembered "only through the eyes of all the forgotten others":

on Monday a cat in the sorceresses' alley
screeched out your death
in another year's language
and I had forgotten
your name
like the promise of hunger.

The incisiveness of the language is hobbled by the sibilance of "sorceresses' alley" making the reader pause to puzzle out its meaning only to collide with the onomatopoeia of "screeched" and be hit by a stunning announcement of "your death." That the person addressed is a former lover is not certain. It seems she is a woman with whom the speaker had a close relationship in "the old days." Memory is as inevitable as hunger. So, the speaker, having "never remained" in the proscribed world of the female invert, is nonetheless forced to recall the hell of "the old days" and to confront anew her purposeful forgetting. "Everyone wants to know how / it was / in the old days," the opening lines of the last stanza, are symmetrical with the those of the first stanza, signaling the speaker's need to remember the hell of "the old days;" and not to be seduced into forgetting that "the old days" were days of insatiable emotional hunger, repressed sex, and public censure. Unlike the speaker in "Artisan" who seems to objectify her beloved and set herself apart, this speaker joins with those "forgotten others" to claim a forgotten agency.

Throughout her life Lorde always gave credit to the women friends and lovers who joined her along the way. "Journeystones I–XI" is a eleven-part poem of tribute to women who mark the speaker's life by what they lack. She greets each woman directly with terse, epigrammatic address, the most direct of which is the following:

> Elaine,
> my sister outsider
> I still salute
> the power of learning
> loss. (102)

The last three lines of "Elaine" could perhaps underscore Lorde's life work. However, the lyrics to "Maxine," "China," "Jan," "Margaret," "Catherine," "Isabel," "Joyce," "Janie," and "Flora," the other addressees, give more play to the sardonic and sarcastic, the most savage of which is Maxine's:

> Maxine
> I used to admire your talent
> for saying nothing

so well
that way the blood
was always someone else's
and there was always
someplace left
to be yourself
the stranger

More than a tallying of emotional conquests or an act of divination, "Journeystones" exposes the poet's demonic virtuosity. "China" is a "girl on the run." "Jan," to whom Lorde has spoken before in this collection, is a name for "so many people / I cannot remember" (103). "Margaret," also spoken to before, is a "prehistoric nut." "Catherine" is a "little pungent onion," incapable of intimacy. "Isabel" is a friend who "hurt[s] and lean[s] / at the same time." "Joyce" is "furious / and without anyone / to kill." "Janie" is "dangerous as coral." And finally, "Flora" is interested in masochism: "If you make me stone / I will bruise you."

As if anticipating the reader's impatience with the metaphorical casting of stones, the speaker implicates herself in the others' failings, while still remaining distant herself from the objects of her derision: "The last hole in fortune / is the anger of the empress / knowing herself as mortal / and without child" (104). With the reference to the angry "empress," the speaker draws the focus onto herself so that even her own insufficiency and emptiness can be seen as superior to the others.' Empress indeed.

Lorde's sense of the sacred is primordial, full of sacrifice and expiation befitting her Catholic upbringing, and informed by African and Caribbean figuration. She has always contested Afro-American prescriptions for blackness, particularly those endemic to the Black Arts Movement. Always very formal linguistically, she seems almost to reject Afro-American vernacular speech, which richly informs the writing of most African-

American poets. Black music forms—blues, jazz, spirituals and gospel—do not influence her poetics. I believe she resists more than anything the consolation and the transcendence of the vernacular practices. In Lorde, there is no putting on the robe and walking all over God's heaven; nor any of that hunkering down over one's "missed love" and singing: "There goes my baby movin' on down the road." In the poem "About Religion," however, she reveals a speaker who is an "outsider," but as a child "learned to love / the gospel music" that enveloped her world on Sundays (105). She views the world of black evangelical Christians from the distance of her window above "the garbage cans in the summer / backyards of my childhood." In a rather precious description of the black churchwomen, known as saints, who stand in uniform like stanchions to console the "witnesses" and beat out salvation on tambourines, the speaker reveals her own vulnerability to the rhythms:

> their rocketed beat
> snapped like pea shooters
> in august time
> while the fingered tambourines
> hand heeled beat
> rose through the air shafts
> sweet and timely. (105)

The final image of the speaker's "mother's churchly disapproval" giving way to a grudging regard for the music and those who perform it is another example of how Lorde privileges distance from her subjects, be they lovers or cultures: "A skinny nappy-headed little girl / ran back and forth collecting . . . / coins wrapped in newspapers / and the corner of old sheets."

THE MOST PROBLEMATIC poem for me in this collection is "Power," which Lorde read often at public events in the 1970s and 1980s. Its tone of high moral outrage, its naturalistic description,

its documentary gestures, and its didacticism show its Black Arts
effects. The poem connects quite forcibly with the Black Arts
commitment to, for example, "tell the *truth* to the people" (em-
phasis mine). This poem, then, attempts to "tell the truth" about
the murder of a black child by a white policeman. Though not
named, ten-year-old Clifford Glover is once again the murdered
black child, and for Lorde a gross representation of the physical
and psychic murders all black children suffer on this "desert of
raw gunshot wounds" called North America, sometimes called
"Babylon." A poem of mourning like "Woman/Dirge for Wasted
Children," discussed previously, "Power" does not promise conso-
lation, but rather meditates on the destructive power of rage.
From her usual distance, the speaker instructs the listener in the
following truism, silencing any dissent:

> The difference between poetry and rhetoric
> is being
> ready to kill
> yourself
> instead of your children. (108)

The ambiguity here is maddening, but the weight of the asser-
tion is as unrelenting as Nikki Giovanni's rhetorical challenge,
"Nigger / can you kill?" Is suicide, revenge, revolutionary vio-
lence being implied as that "difference"? Nothing else in
Lorde's poem bears out the above assertion. Like Giovanni and
Sanchez, she critiques the ineffectualness of rhetoric, particu-
larly the bombastic rhetoric of the Black Arts Movement. Po-
etry, seemingly, is a field of action and promises more than just
talk of killing. Documentable quotations from the trial of the
"37-year-old white man with 13 years of police forcing" and
references to the jury of eleven white men and one black
woman that set him free are inserted between two cataclysmic
visions. In the first vision, the speaker sees that "a dead child is
dragging his shattered black / face off the edge of my sleep"

(108), while she tries to "make power out of hatred and de-struction." In the second and final vision, in a gesture reminis-cent of the Black Arts Movement, the speaker uses her inconsolable rage as a threat, allowing it to fuel a dream of re-venge against as defenseless a target as the ten-year-old child:

> and one day I will take my teenaged plug
> and connect it to the nearest socket
> raping an 85-year-old white woman
> who is somebody's mother
> and as I beat her senseless and set a torch to her bed
> a greek chorus will be singing in 3/4 time
> 'Poor thing. She never hurt a soul. What beasts they
>   are.' (109)

Especially when one has the power of words, "Power" is an ex-ample of how difficult feeling powerless is, how difficult to con-trol the rhetoric of subjection, and how difficult to mediate the use of anger as an instrument of action. The poem struggles to be that difference between poetry and rhetoric.

"Between Ourselves," at one time the name of a chapbook by Lorde, is an exquisite and angry response to the prescriptive-ness of black nationalism. The speaker rejects unitary blackness as the only signifier of community. Instead of creating community, "the rooms full of black faces" would destroy her for any differ-ence. She exposes the reduction of racial heritage to "easy black-ness" by offering the narrative of her great grandmother who was sold into slavery by a black man. Rejecting race as the sole basis of affinity and unity, she refuses the fictions used to justify this longing for racial purity in the following twice repeated chorus:

> I do not believe
> our wants
> have made all our lies
> holy. (112, 113)

Still meditating upon the color of her great grandmother's betrayal, she eschews calling upon the orishas, "Shopona," god of disease, and "Orishala," the god who gives shape to human beings in the womb, to reckon with "that brother" (112). Once again, the poem turns on Lorde's belief that hatred of the other is hatred of oneself. All black people have in common their internalization of white culture, "consumed in secret / before we were born," that is, before "we" were converted to "Blackness." Here she warns against the reenactment of her great grandmother's betrayal:

> When you impale me
> upon your lances of narrow blackness
> before you hear my heart speak
> mourn your own borrowed blood
> your own borrowed visions. . . .
> we are all children of Eshu

In the final poem of the collection, "Solstice," a poem of transition bespeaking the urgency of new birth, the speaker vows to "eat the last signs of my weakness / remove the scars of old childhood wars" (117). This poem, enunciated in a litany of negatives, is troubled, so typical of Lorde's refusal to resolve, but mundane upon comparison with other splendid poems in the collection:

> May I never remember reasons
> for my spirit's safety
> may I never forget
> the warning of my woman's flesh
> weeping at the new moon
> may I never lose
> that terror
> that keeps me brave
> May I owe nothing
> that I cannot repay. (118)

The Black Unicorn is a book of disturbances. It disturbs the patriarchal cosmos of Afro-American poetry, though certainly not the only text by a black woman during this time that does so. It, however, is the only text that disrupts the uncomplicated poetic confluence black nationalism maintained with Africa, the Caribbean, and North America. *The Black Unicorn* continues Lorde's feminist conversations in *From A Land Where Other People Live* and *New York Head Shop and Museum* and offers a diasporic poetics that challenges the "protectionist" values of the Afro-American literary landscape. Lorde paves the way for a generation of black feminist and lesbian feminist writers to create a literary movement challenging black nationalist orthodoxy and white feminist exclusion to say nothing of patriarchy.

The years from 1979 to 1990—despite Reagan and Bush—allowed watershed writing for women of color feminists, particularly lesbian feminists. Barbara Smith and Lorraine Bethel coedited *Conditions: Five, the Black Women's Issue.*[11] *Conditions: Five* featured for the first time in the history of Afro-American literary strivings the work of self-identified black lesbian writers. However, Toni Cade Bambara's previously discussed anthology, *The Black Woman*, was the first collection of writings by black women with feminist leanings and gave impetus to *Conditions: Five.* Though most Black Arts Movement projects were no longer in high evidence by 1979, in their introduction to the issue the coeditors cite the lingering perils of writing as a feminist or a lesbian "within" or "without" the circle of prescriptive/proscriptive blackness:

> In choosing from the work that was submitted we placed a priority on writing concerning itself with the issues of feminism and lesbianism as they related to Black women. Our major reason for this standard comes from the belief that anti-feminism and homophobia in the Black community make it difficult, if not impossible, for Black women to

publish lesbian/feminist writing in the traditional Black media. (12)

Though the histories vary on how it began and who began it, Smith and Cherríe Moraga were instrumental in establishing Kitchen Table: Women of Color Press, and Audre Lorde served as a member of its all-women-of-color editorial collective. Kitchen Table published two critical feminist anthologies; each carved out the province of women of color, primarily lesbian of color, politics and poetics: *This Bridge Called My Back: Writings by Radical Women of Color*,[12] edited by Moraga and the late Gloria Anzaldua in 1983, to which Toni Cade Bambara wrote the "Foreword"; and *Home Girls: A Black Feminist Anthology*, edited by Smith, and an expansion of *Conditions: Five, the Black Women's Issue*. Audre Lorde's prose, not her poetry, appeared in both of these anthologies. Lorde's often-quoted article, "The Master's Tools Will Never Dismantle The Master's House" and "An Open Letter To Mary Daly," Lorde's notorious critique of Daly's Euro-centered appraisal of "women's ecology," appeared in *This Bridge Called My Back*; and "Tar Beach," which was part of Lorde's biomythography, *Zami: A New Spelling of My Name*, appeared in *Home Girls*, as it had in *Conditions: Five* in 1979.

Even before the publication of her poem "Who Said It Was Simple," one of the earliest theorizings on the simultaneity of oppressions, Audre Lorde theorized as early as 1968 about the intersections of race and gender and the pervasiveness of race and gender oppression, in her fourteen-line epigram, "Revolution Is One Form of Social Change," though it was not published until 1973 in *New York Headshop and Museum*. Her outsider identity, more than any other of the multiplicity of who she was, empowered her never to become settled into anyone's notion of stable identity, even as she insisted upon her "lesbian feminist" positionality.

BLACK WOMEN POETS AND
THE PUBLIC: A CONCLUSION
FOR NOW

The Black Arts Movement projected a prescriptive practice
of "Black American culture" and a prescriptive remaking of the
souls of black folk because of what was perceived as a self-re-
demptive need for political and cultural power in an antiblack,
racist country. I have described the Black Arts Movement as a
circle of compatriots, with standards of membership and expec-
tations of performance—standards and expectations circum-
scribed and inflected by gender and heterosexuality. In his 1968
article, "The Black Arts Movement," Larry Neal positions black
power (as political theory) with the undifferentiated black pub-
lic, which he assigns to the tutelage of the "Black artist," whose
referent is always masculine and who destroys—in the counter-
public arena—the black/white binary in service to both the
politics and aesthetics of blackness. The black writer/artist, him-
self/herself, was called upon to "break with the literary main-
stream," according to Hoyt W. Fuller, and to seal the break
between literature and life (199) with his/her own funky body.

Black women poets within the circle actively participated
in the "nation/institution-building," a requisite for membership.
Poets—for example, Giovanni, Sanchez, Rodgers, Cortez—self-
published or published with independent presses, like Broad-
side, in the early days of the Movement. They were teachers in
new black studies programs in predominantly white universi-
ties—and remained so; Sanchez recently retired from Temple
University, Cortez left Rutgers in the 1980s, and Giovanni still
teaches at Virginia Tech. They considered themselves Black
Power advocates and activists. Margaret Danner, Gwendolyn
Brooks, and Naomi Long Madgett were long-time poets of the
Midwest (Chicago and Detroit) who had been involved with
poetry since the 1940s. Brooks underwrote a number of Broad-

side's 1970 publications. A member of that same workshop with Inez Stark to which Brooks belonged in the 1940s, Margaret Danner, was also a journal editor and supporter of the new black poetry. Naomi Long Madgett was a founder and publisher of another independent book company, Lotus Press of Detroit, which published poetry. Black women's poetry, like that of black men, was expected to provide a "series of easy-to-follow thematic road maps to both personal and group empowerment" (Van Deburg 290). And it did. Tasks included aiding in the "Negro to Black" conversion, deploying black vernacular practices, especially language and music, recovering the African and the Afro-American past, creation of a communal and cross-class culture, observing the "functions" (men) and "graces" (women) of gender, and making the revolution, the more literal, the better.

Different from the subtle tactics of revision employed by New Negro Renaissance women poets, women poets of the Black Arts Movement deployed multiple voices of recovery, reclamation, and revision and threw off the sex and gender constraints of their foresisters. Black Arts women's poetry represented their concerns as race people to the yet-to-be-converted, imagined community of black people as well as that imagined community already within the circle. Black male critics of the time found it difficult to represent the more volatile poetry of black women because of their need to stabilize a kind of lyric voice in the women poets, which they could no longer use in their own poetry, because of the "race's" race to manhood.

In his 1969 antimodernist tour de force "Black Art," Amiri Baraka radically redefines poetry as visceral ungendered life, "Poems are bullshit unless they are / teeth or trees" (*Transbluesency* 142). This redefinition of poetry is also a redefinition of blackness in which the death of whiteness is explicit. Baraka theorizes further: "We want poems that kill. / Assassin poems.

Poems that shoot / guns." Baraka here exemplifies a critical piece of Black Arts literacy: the enunciation of fighting words.

> You ain't never far away
> enough to not
> need
> the blues
>   (Morris 4)

The taking of public space by Black Arts poets and their schooling on the "Black" word are realized anew in the current spoken word/performance poetry as well as hip hop and rap music. In *Black Noise: Rap Music and Black Culture in Contemporary America*, Tricia Rose devotes an important chapter to "Bad Sistuhs," black women rappers, whom she theorizes are "carving out a female dominated space in which black women's sexuality is openly expressed" (170). However, like the space carved out by women poets of the Black Arts Movement, that space is circumscribed by a black heterosexual male political agenda, intensified by the commodification of rap and hip-hop. Rose muses that race is still a point of confluence for black men and black women, demonstrated by the women rappers' resistance to being cast in opposition to the male rappers. This resistance, Rose continues, is exemplified in their reluctance to characterize their work as feminist, mostly because of what they perceive are feminism's connections to whiteness, and, I might add, women rappers' fear of rejection by the brothers.

Women rappers, like the women poets of the Black Arts Movement, have a dialogic relationship with their male counterparts, in which their raps often critique the sexism of male raps. However, outside the discursive space of rap, few women rappers criticize their male colleagues' sexist expressions or actions. Of course, developments in poetry by Afro-Americans are not always symmetrical with developments in Afro-American music, especially the more mainstream of black music. Black

Arts poetry rejected the commodifying demands of mainstream culture as does black lesbian feminism. Yet, I think black rap as well as the Black Arts Movement poetry as well as black lesbian feminist poetry—with their similar and different influences—demonstrate most black women's longing for cross–gender-racial ties, including black lesbians. Much lesbian feminist poetry rejects patriarchal conventions, just as the Black Arts Movement poetry rejects white/Western conventions and, by implication, white patriarchy.

The Black Arts Movement women poets proclaimed, "I am a Black woman," privileging race as precedent and the primary category of struggle. Open heterosexuality was also the only sexual option for women (and men) in the circle of the Black Arts Movement, as Sonia Sanchez's 1966 poem "to all sisters" proclaims: "there ain't / no MAN like a / black man" (Jones and Neal, eds. 255).

The intertextual relationships of black nationalist poetry and black lesbian-feminist poetry reenact themselves through-out the 1970s into the mid-1980s. Also, in the 1980s, the voices of black lesbian feminist writers are joined by the voices of black gay men, such as Essex Hemphill, Melvin Dixon, editor Joseph Beam, filmmakers Isaac Julien and Marlon Riggs—satisfying in one way the desire for cross–gender-racial ties. Of course, the scourge of AIDS also solidified the alliances between black lesbians and gay men.

While the Black Arts Movement reified heterosexuality and nation, black and white lesbian-feminist poets venerated lesbian sexuality and lesbian culture. Feminism was not lost on the Black Arts Movement women poets, nor was black autonomy lost on black lesbian feminists. Even those nonfeminist women who remained for a time within the circle of the Black Arts Movement offered coded critiques of the sexism of black men, as in Sanchez's "blk/rhetoric" and Giovanni's "Seduction" and "True Import." Longings for racial acceptance and exclusivity were transferred to the writings of black lesbian feminists as demonstrated in "The Combahee River Collective Statement," in terms of its failure to critique homophobia in the black community and thereby run less of a risk of being rejected because of its already enunciated black feminism. Lorraine Bethel's 1979 poem, "What Chou Mean We, White Girl," appearing in *Conditions: Five, The Black Women's Issue*, critiques the tokenism in the lesbian feminist movement and is a very bitter comment on the material privilege of white women and their institutions—from "Volvos" to "health centers"—vis-à-vis the virtual lack of resources, which often limited black women's participation in movement culture (88).

However, to counter the persistence with male dominance and the obsession with heterosexuality and its conventions, black women writers had to move outside the circle of male-centered blackness as we see with the poems (and lives) of Audre Lorde, Ntozake Shange, Alice Walker, June Jordan. Pat Parker, a transplanted Texan living in the Oakland, California, had been writing antisexist and antiracist poetry since 1961. "Where Will You Be," appearing in 1979 in *Conditions: Five*, seems nearly prophetic given the current Christian Right campaign against gays and lesbians. Yet, the poem does not recommend the taking up of arms to fend off the enemy, as do Giovanni's "True Import" and many other Black Arts texts. It dissolves into a catalogue of paradoxes revolving around gays' and lesbians' "perversity" in allowing themselves to be coerced into silence, into the closet, into not defending their human rights: "Everytime we put on the proper / clothes to go to a family / wedding and left our lovers / at home— / it was an act of perversion" (76). And as "True Import" castigates the "nigger" for being unready for killing, "Where Will You Be" castigates the "homosexual . . . faggot . . . lesbian . . . dyke . . . gay . . . queer" for believing assimilation will protect them from the "Chains and locks." Years before black lesbian writers developed a voice, homophobia in the black political community was evidenced in poetry and theatre. Most writers discussed in this book, have widened the lenses of their poetry beyond the strictly domestic racial perspective and have adopted diasporic, feminist/womanist, international perspectives, though blackness remains a powerful store of knowledge and creativity.

Inside or outside the circle of blackness, inside or outside the space of feminism and lesbian-feminism, black women poets complicated that turbulent landscape from 1968 to 1978. It is sometimes difficult for black feminist and lesbian-feminist writers to admit their debt to the Black Arts Movement because of its misogyny, heterosexism, and homophobia. Also difficult for black lesbian-feminists is admitting solidarity with white lesbian-feminists because of the longing for racial solidarity with the black community and the long history of white racism. Black poetry of the seventies mourns the loss of possibility for confluence in the aftermath of the sixties' social and cultural revolutions.

Though intensely critical of all manner of nationalisms and separatisms, I have a personal investment in writing about Black Arts poetry. I was forever transformed by it and have always wanted to make a contribution to the field of black poetry and black American writing—as poet and as critic. In the epigraph to this section from the poem, "Get Away 1928," of spoken word and slam artist, Tracie Morris, "the blues" here is that rootedness and rootlessness in black culture, as a living testament to its deep resources for all of us as poets, as citizens, as cultural workers and warriors—black and all colors. It is the "practice of black American culture" that Bernice Reagan speaks of as needing to be learned through exposing oneself to risk—the risk of "missed love," of suffering—perhaps even to die, as many people did during the Civil Rights Movement of the 1960s, the Black Power Movement of the 1970s, and the final struggle against Apartheid in South Africa of the 1980s.

Rereading this poetry gives me new courage to address the commodifying aspects of mainstream culture, but not for a millisecond to think that I am immune to its effects. The shift toward independent cultural institutions, particularly the print enterprises, among Black Arts practitioners and later among lesbian feminists, created powerful poetry legacies that may still enable and sustain our communities and motivate progressive action.

Notes

INTRODUCTION 'AFTER MECCA'

1. However, within the last eighteen years, critical work has been pro-
duced on the poetry of African American women. Akasha (Gloria)
Hull's book on the women poets of the Harlem Renaissance, *Color,
Sex, and Poetry: Three Women Writers of the Harlem Renaissance* (1987)
places Georgia Douglas Johnson, Alice Dunbar Nelson, Angelina
Weld Grimké on the literary map. Indeed, Hull began to address
black women poets even earlier in her groundbreaking article,
"Buried Under the Days" (*Conditions: Five, the Black Women's Issue,*
1979) which recovered the life and work of Grimké and discovered
the same-gender beloved in her sonnets. Also in 1987 Doris Daven-
port produced her dissertation, "Four Contemporary Black Women
Poets: Lucille Clifton, June Jordan, Audre Lorde, and Sherley Anne
Williams (A Feminist Study of a Culturally Derived Poetics)." Of
course, Alicia Suskin Ostriker's *Stealing the Language: The Emergence
of Women's Poetry in America* (1986) is an exhaustive study of women
poets and integrates references to Wheatley, Grimké, Georgia Doug-
las Johnson, Anne Spencer, and contemporary poets such as Clifton,
Sonia Sanchez, Nikki Giovanni, Audre Lorde, and so on. "Living on
the Line: Audre Lorde and *Our Dead Behind Us*" in *Changing Our
Own Words: Essays on Criticism, Theory, and Writing by Black Women*
(Wall, ed. 1989) represents another groundbreaking treatment by
Hull of a complex black woman poet. Anthologies such as *Black Sis-
ter: Poetry by Black American Women, 1746–1980*, edited by Erlene
Stetson (1981), and *Shadowed Dreams: Women's Poetry of the Harlem
Renaissance*, edited by Maureen Honey (1989) are valuable contri-
butions to the field. More recently, some studies have begun to
address the absence of critical treatments of poetry by black women
and other women of color: Betsy Erkkila's *The Wicked Sisters:
Women Poets, Literary History* (1992) includes a chapter on Gwen-
dolyn Brooks; Kim Whitehead's *The Feminist Poetry Movement*
(1996) includes a chapter on June Jordan and references to Lorde,
California Black lesbian poet, Pat Parker, Nikki Giovanni, Sonia
Sanchez; AnaLouise Keating's *Women Reading Women Writing:*

Self-Invention in Paula Gunn Allen, Gloria Anzaldua, and Audre Lorde (1996) addresses these three writers as products of a movement that gave voice to lesbian of color poets. In 1999, Fahamisha Shariat Brown published *The Performed Word*, which addresses the contributions of contemporary black women poets to the vernacular culture of African Americans. In 1982, lesbian poet Jan Clausen wrote a little-known monograph, *A Movement of Poets: Thoughts on Poetry and Feminism*, which critiqued the static definitions of women's poetry emerging at that time from the lesbian-feminist movement and charted the development of the women's publishing institutions. Clausen discusses many black women poets, lesbian and nonlesbian, whose work influenced the lesbian poetry-writing community.

CHAPTER 1 'MISSED LOVE'

1. Dudley Randall was dubbed "father of the new black poetry" by *Black Enterprise Magazine* in 1978. More than that, Randall, as his friend Naomi Long Madgett writes, is "a pioneer in independent African-American publishing. . . . [whose publications] changed the whole character of American literature." Born in Washington, D.C., in 1914, Randall moved to Detroit in 1920. His first poem was published in the *Detroit Free Press* when he was thirteen; he became librarian and poet in residence at the University of Detroit in 1969 and was proclaimed Poet Laureate of Detroit by Mayor Coleman Young in 1981. He received a Lifetime Achievement Award from the National Endowment for the Arts in 1996. After continued bouts with depression, Randall sold the Press to Hilda and Don Vest in 1985, who maintained it as a cultural institution, keeping many of his titles in press, for example, Sonia Sanchez's *Homecoming* (1969), Audre Lorde's *From A Land Where Other People Live* (1973), and Etheridge Knight's *Poems From Prison* (1968). In 2000, the Vests donated the archives of Broadside to the Special Collections Library of the University of Michigan. Dudley Randall died on August 5, 2000 (Naomi Long Madgett, "Dudley Randall's Life and Career." August 15, 2000. July 31, 2003<http://www.english.uiuc. edu/maps/poets/m_r/randall/life.html>.) Between 1965 and 1984, Broadside produced more than two hundred black poets in broadsides, individual collections, anthologies, records and tapes, in addition to those named above are Nikki Giovanni, Haki Madhubuti, Gwendolyn Brooks, Amiri Baraka, Carolyn Rodgers, Melvin Dixon, Margaret Danner, Sterling Brown, Everett Hoagland, Randall himself, and numerous less well-known poets. Broadside Press is a cultural marker of an epic generation. (During its heyday, I collected many of its publications and still possess them today.)

2. The two words, black power, were first used as a mobilizing slogan by Willie Ricks and Carmichael. "It was a call for blacks to unite,

lead their own organizations, and reject racist institutions of American society." Ricks joined SNCC as a high school student in the early 1960s. "A self-described nationalist . . . he shortened the slogan 'Black Power for Black People' to the popular 'Black Power.'" See Greenberg, ed., *Circle of Trust: Remembering SNCC* (New Brunswick, N.J.: Rutgers University Press, 1998), 203. Not a call to nationalism, "Black Power" galvanized black activists who were disillusioned with nonviolence as a strategy. Martin Luther King describes this moment in his memoir, *Where Do We Go From Here* (1966): "At a huge mass meeting that night . . . Stokely mounted the platform and after arousing the audience with a powerful attack on Mississippi justice, he proclaimed: 'What we need is black power.' Willie Ricks, the fiery orator of SNCC, leaped to the platform and shouted, 'What do you want?' The crowd roared, 'Black Power.' Again and again Ricks cried, 'What do you want?' and the response 'Black Power' grew louder and louder, until it had reached fever pitch." See James M. Washington, ed., *The Essential Writings and Speeches of Martin Luther King* (New York: HarperCollins Publishers, 1991), 573–574. King does not mention that Carmichael had been arrested earlier in the day and had attended the rally after spending six hours in jail. Later Carmichael admitted to King that he had manipulated his participation in the march to give the Black Power concept a "'national forum.'" Carson recounts that Carmichael "was the last speaker of the rally" and "still angered by his arrest . . . told an audience . . . 'This is the twenty-seventh time I have been arrested. I ain't going to jail no more . . . . What we gonna start saying now is 'black power!' He shouted the slogan repeatedly; each time the audience shouted back, 'black power!' Willie Ricks leaped to the platform and asked, 'What do you want?' Again and again the audience shouted in unison the slogan that had suddenly galvanized their emotions." See *In Struggle: SNCC and the Black Awakening of the 1960's* (1981; 2d ed., Cambridge, Mass.: Harvard University Press, 1981), 210.

3. In the years since Jones/Baraka wrote this essay, Wheatley has been evaluated differently. Writers and scholars as varied as Alice Walker "In Search of Our Mother's Gardens," (*Ms.* 1974), Barbara Johnson "Euphemisim, Understatement, and the Passive Voice: Genealogy of African-American Poetry," in *The Feminist Difference: Literature, Psychoanalysis, Race, and Gender* (Cambridge, Mass.: Harvard University Press, 1998); June Jordan "The Difficult Miracle of Black Poetry in America or Something Like a Sonnet for Phillis Wheatley," in *On Call* (Boston, Mass.: South End Press, 1985); Henry Louis Gates "Phillis Wheatley and 'The Nature of the Negro,'" in *Figures in Black: Words Signs, and the "Racial" Self* (New York: Oxford University Press, 1987) and *The Trials of Phillis Wheatley: Americas First Black Poet and Her Encounters with the Founding Fathers* (New York: Basic

Books, 2003) have vindicated Wheatley and her work. In both *Figures* and *Signifying Monkey: A Theory of African-American Literary Criticism* (New York: Oxford, 1988), Gates attacks Jones/Baraka and other Black Arts/Black Aesthetic proponents who "define the principles of [literary] criticism upon which a 'genuinely black' aesthetic could be posited" (*Figures*, xxv).

4. In "Query XIV: Laws" of his dense and historic *Notes on the State of Virginia*, published in 1785, Jefferson ruminates at length on the differences in the races, with particular attention to physical and intellectual differences. He queries his readers: "Are not the fine mixtures of red and white, the expressions of every passion by greater of less suffusions of color in the one, preferable to that eternal monotony, which reigns in the countenances, that immoveable veil of black which covers all the emotions of the other race?" (139). Ruminating further, Jefferson does give blacks credit for the ability to learn, to speak, and to sing: "But never yet could I find that a black had uttered a thought above the level of plain narration; never see even an elementary trait of painting or sculpture. In music they are more generally gifted than the whites with accurate ears for tune and time, and they have been found capable of imagining a small catch. . . . Misery is often the parent of the most affecting touches in poetry. Among blacks is misery enough, God knows, but no poetry. . . . Their love is ardent, but it kindles the senses only, not the imagination. Religion indeed has produced a Phyllis Whately [sic]; but it could not produce a poet. The compositions published under her name are below the dignity of criticism. The heroes of the Dunciad are to her, as Hercules to the author of that poem" (140).

5. Jones/Baraka was not the first black writer to criticize black literary production in the United States as pandering to white tastes; I discussed earlier that he was not the first man to criticize Wheatley for her presumed inauthenticity. Richard Wright's "Blueprint for Negro Writing" (1937), which appeared in *New Challenge*, was even more damning and certainly more didactic: "Generally speaking, Negro writing in the past has been confined to humble novels, poems, and plays, prim and decorous ambassadors who went a-begging to white America. . . . Under these conditions Negro writing assumed two general aspects: (1) It became a sort of conspicuous ornamentation, the hallmark of 'achievement.' (2) It became the voice of the educated Negro pleading with white Americans for justice;" see Angelyn Mitchell, ed., *Within The Circle: An Anthology of African American Literary Criticism From The Harlem Renaissance to The Present* (Durham: Duke University Press, 1994), 97–98.

6. *The Journal of Black Poetry* was established in San Francisco in the spring of 1966 by Joe Goncalves, who stated that it "is published for black people everywhere . . . [and] will appear quarterly." It pub-

lished only black male poets until the issue referenced above in the fall of 1967. Women poets published were Sonia Sanchez, Gwendolyn Brooks, and Jewel Latimore. It is an important historical publication for its direct history of the black arts crusade, of its principal participants, their theories of art, and their positions on society and politics. Production values were always rather low on this publication. The major (male) articulators of the Black Aesthetic appeared within its thin covers: Marvin Jackmon (aka Marvin X), Ed Bullins, Clarence Major, LeRoi Jones, Dudley Randall, Sam Cornish, Don L. Lee, Larry Neal, and so on. The issues included translations of Césaire, David Diop, reprints of Garvey, Pushkin. "Let there be blackness over this land. / Let Black Power shine and shine" was the motto of its first issue.

7. Rodgers's discussion of the technique of "signifying," though more immediately reflective of the practice of the dozens, opens the space twenty years later for Henry Louis Gates, Jr.'s pathbreaking study *Signifying Monkey: A Theory of African-American Literary Criticism*, in which Yoruba hermeneutics becomes a discursive site for the development of African-American critical practice. Rodgers's use of "signifying" and Gates's use of "Signifyin(g)" have—as Gates says of the black vernacular "Signification" and the standard English "signification"—"everything to do with one another and, then again, absolutely nothing" (45). Rodgers sees the "signifying" poem as a way of "making love to—while poking fun at—one's self and one's lifestyles," and Gates, informed by post-structuralist theorists, sees "signifying" as the practice of paying homage to and critiquing African American literary culture.

8. I am here being less expansive on the relationship between black music and black poetry during this era than I would like. If I did, this would be a different book. But I return to the notion of "missed love." However, since 1990 several important books have been written to consider the constitutive relationship between African American popular music (rock 'n' roll, rhythm and blues, soul, hip-hop) and the politics of African American communities, particularly the communities' post–World War II disappointment, bitterness, sense of loss, and hurt, that the promises of democracy have resulted in broken dreams and stifled hopes. Peter Guralnick's *Sweet Soul Music: Rhythm and Blues and the Southern Dream of Freedom* (New York: Little Brown and Company, 1986) pioneers in the telling of music's signification of the Southern Civil Rights Movement, which sought to destroy racial segregation. Martha Bayles's *Hole in Our Soul: The Loss of Beauty and Meaning in American Popular Music* (Chicago: University of Chicago Press, 1994) is more panoramic than specific to soul, R&B, rock 'n roll, etc., but she does offer a necessary critique of the racial politics that governed popular music production from 1955 to 1966. Brian Ward's *Just My Soul*

Responding: Rhythm and Blues, Black Consciousness, and Race Relations (Berkeley, Los Angeles: University of California Press, 1998) argues that black popular music was a ground upon which contestations of black power were staged. Tricia Rose's *Black Noise: Rap Music and Black Culture in Contemporary America* (Hanover: Wesleyan University Press of New England, 1994) examines the impact of rap and hip-hop on contemporary black cultural production and politics in the United States. Suzanne E. Smith's *Dancing in the Street: Motown and the Cultural Politics of Detroit* (Cambridge, Mass.: Harvard University Press, 1999) historicizes Motown in the context of black Detroit, a political and cultural bedrock of the Civil Rights and Black Power movements.

9. Bebop, whose exponents included Charlie "Bird" Parker, Thelonious Monk, Dizzy Gillespie, Betty Carter, Miles Davis, greatly influenced the New Music of the sixties, some of whose chief exponents were Sun Ra, John Coltrane, Pharoah Sanders, Yusef Lateef, Archie Shepp, the Art Ensemble of Chicago, to name only the more well known and mostly East Coast players. Countless Black Arts poems try to emulate Coltrane's "sheets of sound" that revolutionized the performance of jazz, notably Don L. Lee's "Don't Cry, Scream (for John Coltrane/from a black poet/in a basement apt. crying dry tears of 'you ain't gone.')," in which Lee embellishes the long "e" sound of "scream" in emulation of Coltrane's amelodic heights on tenor and soprano saxophones.

10. Representative titles include *Black on Black* by Black Student Union of Stanford University, 1967; Hayden, ed., *Kaleidoscope: Poems by American Negro Poets*, 1967; Jones and Neal, eds., *Black Fire: An Anthology of Afro-American Writing*, 1968; Alhamisi and Wangara, eds., *Black Arts: An Anthology of Black Creations*, 1969; Jordan, ed., *Souscript: Afro-American Poetry,* 1970; Giovanni, ed., *Night Comes Softly: Anthology of Black Female Voices*, 1970; Baker, ed., *Black Literature in America*, 1971; Brooks, ed., *A Broadside Treasury*, 1971; Barksdale and Kinnamon, eds., *Black Writers of America: A Comprehensive Anthology*, 1972; Adoff, ed., *The Poetry of Black America: Anthology of the 20th Century*, 1973; Henderson, ed., *Understanding the New Black Poetry: Black Speech and Poetic References*, 1973; the reprinting and revision of Bontemps, ed., *American Negro Poetry*, 1963, 1974; Cannon, ed., *Jumbalaya*, 1975.

11. According to the introductory essay to Hayden's poetry in the *Norton Anthology of African-American Literature*, "Hayden's art—subtle, intellectual, firmly situated in the academy—was not what the young black nationalists had in mind [at the 1966 Black Writers Conference at Fisk University], mainly because it did not promote an aesthetic that furthered the cause of black revolution, and they did not hold back from saying so. . . . Hayden refused to be pressured," in Gates et al., 1498.

CHAPTER 2   THE LOSS OF LYRIC SPACE IN GWENDOLYN
BROOKS'S "IN THE MECCA"

1. This chapter appeared in a slightly different version as an article in
the Winter issue of the *Kenyon Review* (1995), pp. 136–147.
2. Robert F. Williams was head of the Monroe, North Carolina, chap-
ter of the NAACP in 1960. According to Carson's *In Struggle*,
Williams "had become the center of a national controversy because
of his advocacy of armed self-defense by blacks. He actively re-
cruited working-class blacks into the NAACP who supported not
only his position on self-defense but also his demands [to the
county government] for employment opportunities and for deseg-
regation" (42). After a bitter and brutal desegregation campaign,
Williams fled Monroe to avoid trumped-up charges of kidnapping.
He eventually escaped to Cuba for a long period of exile"(43). See
his book, *Negroes With Guns*.
3. "Négritude . . . is used to describe a [social and political] movement
in the arts toward the articulation of the African experience in the
world. . . . [It] reaffirms African cultural traditions, and resists the
European attitudes, beliefs, and traditions forced upon Africans
during periods of colonial rule. . . . In its strictest definition, the
concept of Négritude advances the idea that black Africans have
qualitatively different experiences in the world. They share among
themselves a psychological experience of 'blackness' denied to other
peoples." Its essentialist doctrine has been roundly criticized by
many black intellectuals and scholars, and so has its sexism, as Brent
Hayes Edwards points out: "The narrative of the emergence of
Négritude has been a story of 'representative colored men': Seng-
hor, Leon-Gontran Damas, and Aimé Césaire. The symbology of
the movement is sung not only through Léopold Sédar Senghor's
hymns to the 'Black Woman' (*Femme Noire*), but equally through a
range of commentary on the black woman's role that systematically
overlooks the direct contribution of women like [Paulette] Nardal
to the movement's emergence" in *The Practice of Diaspora: Literature,
Translation, and the Rise of Black Internationalism* (Cambridge, Mass.:
Harvard University Press, 2003), pp. 120–121. Négritude "sparked a
[literary] revolution throughout Africa and among African Ameri-
cans as well" in Appia and Gates, eds., *The Dictionary of Global Cul-
ture* (New York: Knopf, 1996), 480.

CHAPTER 3   QUEEN SISTUH

1. I wish to take this opportunity to thank Professor Eleanor Traylor
of Howard University for the inspiration to explore Douglass's the-
ory of being "within" and "without" the circle of blackness. I sat in
on her graduate seminar, "The Black Arts Movement," to share my

work. Professor Traylor and her students explicated the passage from Douglass as prefatory to their discussion of Afro-American literary theory.

2. Baraka has been roundly criticized by black critics of Afro-American literature since he wrote the piece for its callous dismissal of black literary traditions predating 1965, the birth of the Black Arts Movement. Gates, Jr., patently dislikes Baraka, incessantly citing both in *Figures* and the epic *Signifying Monkey* Ellison's "signifying" comment on Baraka's *Blues People*. Looking back on this era, Gates charges that "race as the controlling mechanism in critical theory reached its zenith of influence and mystification when LeRoi Jones metamorphosed himself into Imamu Baraka and his dashiki-clad, Swahili-named 'habari gani' disciples 'discovered' they were black"(31). In an overlong article, entitled "Contemporary Afro-American Poetry As Folk Art," written eleven years after Baraka's "Myth of a Negro Literature," Bernard Bell complains that "Wright's ['Blue Print for a Negro Literature'] had a much more dramatic influence on the revolutionary commitment of Black nationalist writers of the sixties. This is most clearly evidenced in the cultural nationalism of Imamu Amiri Baraka. In 'The Myth of a 'Negro Literature,' Baraka updates and refocuses Wright's blueprint for Black writers. Intemperately attacking the whole corpus of Afro-American literature, Baraka asks: 'Where is the Negro-ness of a literature written in imitation of the meanest of social intelligences to be found in American culture, i.e., the white middle class?'" See *Black World* (March, 22, no. 5, 1973),19.

3. Jones and Neal's *Black Fire*, published in 1968, one of the earliest anthologies of the era, purports to be "An Anthology of Afro-American Writing." It is, rather, an anthology of predominantly Afro-American men's writing. All fourteen theoreticians/essayists are men. Three of the fifty poets are women. Two of the seven fiction writers are women. And one of the ten playwrights is a woman. *The New Black Poetry* (1969) is slightly less egregious in its representation, with its editor Clarence Major boasting in his introduction that: "For the first time in *any* anthology, to my knowledge, here is a fair representation of female poets" (20). Of the seventy-five poets published "here," twelve are women; that is still less than one-fifth of the poets. Yes, one wonders just exactly what Major meant by "fair representation" in this quite influential book of quite mediocre poetry. He most certainly cannot mean equitable; he must mean tolerable or passable. However, the women's poems do offer a fair representation of the concerns male editors preferred to publish during this era: longing for Africa, motherhood, black history, rearing of children in blackness, understanding of black roots, rejection of whiteness. In 1971, Gwendolyn Brooks edited another influential anthology called *A Broadside Treasury*, which reprinted in four parts,

poems by all of the Broadside poets as well as those of other practitioners of the new black poetry and the new black consciousness in poetry. It begins with selections from the Randall and Burroughs collection *For Malcolm* (Broadside, 1969), in which poems to Malcolm X by Robert Hayden, LeRoi Jones, Ted Joans, Sonia Sanchez, Larry Neal, and so on are reprinted. The volume ends with reprints from the Broadside publication *Black Poetry: A Supplement to Anthologies Which Exclude Black Poets*, edited by Dudley Randall in 1969 and reprints from Broadside's *Broadside Series*. Unlike the Major anthology, which presented samplings of the new black poetry—that is, one poem per poet—the Brooks anthology presents a more representative sampling of each poet's work in the section called "From the Poets," privileging, however, the work of Nikki Giovanni, Don L. Lee, and Sonia Sanchez over the work of the older generation like Margaret Danner, Margaret Walker, Dudley Randall, and Brooks herself; or of the nationally less well-known of the new poets, like Everett Hoagland, Etheridge Knight, Stephany. Of the forty-five poets presented, one-third are women. The poems of Giovanni, Sanchez, and Lee are allowed more than any other poets to advance the black aesthetic: the experimental lineation, the use of black vernacular language, signifying on backsliding Negroes and blacker-than-thou advocates, allusions to black music and musicians, be-black first provisos, and reject the ways of white folks. Jayne Cortez's work was included in none of these. However, Cortez bears being written more about—both for her radical poetry, her recordings with jazz musicians, and her control of her production. Aldon Nielsen asserts, "Cortez's work, both on the page and on the stage, simply refuses to countenance reductive distinctions between lyric poetry and vernacular song . . . . neither is she willing to concede that avant garde poetry is inaccessible to popular audiences", see *Black Chant: Languages of African-American Postmodernism*.

4. According to Appiah and Gates Jr., eds., *The Dictionary of Global Culture*, 1996, Césaire, Martiniquan poet and inventor of the "neologism" Negritude, wrote his collection of poems, *Cahier D'un Retour Mon Pays Natal (Return to My Native Land)*, in 1947 as he was preparing to return to Martinique in 1947 (124).

5. Carmichael was not reelected as SNCC chairperson. Instead, H. Rap Brown became chair of SNCC in 1967, two years before Giovanni's article. Forman, of course was still involved in the day-to-day running of the organization. As Claybourne Carson states in *In Struggle: SNCC and the Black Awakening of the 1960's*: "Most [of SNCC's staff members] wanted to replace Carmichael with someone less likely to attract the attention of the press. Carmichael himself admitted that he may have taken SNCC 'further than it wanted to go' with his speeches but explained that this was a 'trap' for anyone who would take the chair since the staff had established no

guidelines for its officers. . . . Some believed that Ruby Doris
Robinson could fulfill this role, but she had become debilitated
with a rare form of cancer that would end her life in a few months.
Other SNCC veterans such as Forman were exhausted by the de-
mands placed on them during previous years"(251).

6. Also according to Nielsen, Loftin recorded the poem, "Sunni," as
part of a composition, "Haitian Heritage," by drummer Andrew
Cyrille in 1975. "[Cyrille's] method included the poet as one of the
player-composers. Elouise Loftin is listed and pictured on the album
cover along with the other members of the band Maono, and where
each musician's instrument is specified next to his or her name on
the roster, Loftin is credited simply as 'poet.' . . . In Cyrille's eyes,
then, Loftin was not just a poet brought into the studio for the pur-
pose of reciting to a backdrop of free jamming; she was a cocom-
poser, and her preexisting text, the poem 'Sunni,' was the thematic
material around which Cyrille constructed the first section of his
'Haitian Heritage,' which was entitled 'Voices of the Lineage.'"

7. In 1629, Ben Jonson (1572–1637) wrote an ode, but really an elegy,
entitled "To the Immortal Memory and Friendship of that Noble
Pair, Sir Lucius Cary and Sir H. Morison." Morison was killed in
the Punic Wars in 1629. Jonson wrote the ode on the occasion of
Morison's death. The lines to which I am referring retell the ob-
scure myth of the infant of Saguntum: "Brave infant of Saguntum
. . . . Ere thou wert half got out, / Wise child, didst hastily return, /
And mad'st thy mother's womb thine urn," in G. Parfitt, ed., *The
Complete Poems* (London: Penguin Books, 1988) 212.

8. The counterintelligence program, COINTELPRO, was a coun-
terinsurgency initiative of F.B.I. director J. Edgar Hoover on August
25, 1967, to "'expose, disrupt, misdirect, discredit, or otherwise neu-
tralize the activities of black nationalist, hate-type organizations and
groupings, their leadership, spokesmen, membership, and support-
ers, and to counter their propensity for violence and civil disor-
der.'" Henry Hampton and Steve Fayer, eds., *Voices of Freedom: An
Oral History of the Civil Rights Movement from the 1950' through the
1980's* (New York: Bantam Books, 1990), 511–512. Rather like
Homeland Security and the Patriot Act.

Chapter 4 Black Feminist Communalism

1. Hereafter all references to *for colored girls who have considered suicide
when/the rainbow is enuf* appear as *for colored girls*.

2. *The Black Scholar* was established in 1969 and came out six times a
year as a journal of scholarly inquiry of the black world. In 1979
Staples incendiary article caused such a hue and cry among black
intellectuals, especially black women, that *The Black Scholar* editors
dedicated the May/June issue to airing the proverbial dirty laundry

of the sex role debate among the black intelligentsia. A call for responses to Staples article was dispatched and writers, such as Audre Lorde, Kalamu ya Salaam, Pauline Terrelonge Stone, Sabrina Sojourner, Julianne Malveaux, M. Ron Karenga, Askia M. Toure, Alvin Poussaint, Sarah Webster Fabio, June Jordan, Sherley Anne William, and Ntozake Shange herself (submitting two pieces), and Robert Staples himself (responding to the responses), among others, wrote in and were published. In their editorial note prefacing their "Summary of Staples' Article," the editors stated with a feigned equanimity that "Dr. Staples took the recent highly publicized works by Ntozake Shange, *for colored girls who have considered suicide when the rainbow is enuf,* and Michele Wallace, *Black Macho and the Myth of the Superwoman,* as starting points for examining the nature of black sexism" (May/June, 1979, 14). Michele Wallace's work came in for heavy roasting while responses to Shange's *for colored girls* were more even-handed.

3. See Robert B. Stepto's discussion of Johnson's queer novel of racial passing in *From Behind the Veil* (1979). Stepto asserts: "*The Autobiography's* demystification of the 'sacred' bond between Afro-American's music and its tribal integrity is not only part of the 'something,' creating fresh space for the narrative in Afro-American letters, but also a feature anticipating certain prominent tropes and expressions in the literature to come. . . . The Ex-Coloured Man's Club . . . . is catacomb-like and occasionally a setting for intemperance and violence, it is less an inferno and more an Afro-American ritual ground where responses to oppressing social structures are made and in some measure sustained by 'tribal' bonds . . ." (University of Illinois Press, 1991, 122–123).

4. "Reg[u]lar" is another Afro-American vernacular descriptor deployed by Shange. Though other groups have appropriated this descriptor, among black folk in the United States it means a down-to-earth, salt-of-the-earth person (of any "race") who is unpretentious, honest, and gracious.

5. To *read* someone in the Afro-American lexicon of signifying terms, means to reveal some unflattering details about the other in a public setting, while also boasting of one's own power to demean the other.

CHAPTER 5   TRANSFERENCES AND CONFLUENCES

1. This chapter appeared as an article in a 1999 collection of essays edited by Eric Brandt, called *Dangerous Liaisons: Blacks, Gays, and the Struggle for Equality* (New York: The New Press, 1999). The article, "Transferences and Confluences: Black Poetries, the Black Arts Movement, and Black Lesbian Feminism," does not include the examination of Audre Lorde's *Black Unicorn*, but see Alexis De Veaux's

Warrior Poet: A Biography of Audre Lorde (New York: W.W. Norton, 2004) for a rich discussion.

2. I am indebted here to Professor Cheryl A. Wall who defined Audre Lorde's voice as "oracular," that is, possessing a voice whose portent cannot be understood immediately, in a discussion in her graduate seminar, "Black Women Novelists and Critics,"which I was fortunate to audit in 1994.

3. Feminist theorist and cultural critic, Wahneema Lubiano, in her "Black Nationalism and Black Common Sense: Policing Ourselves and Others," in *The House That Race Built: Black Americans, U.S. Terrain*, ed. Lubiano (York: Pantheon Books, 1997) provided me with my adaptation of her theoretical proposition of black nationalism as a common sense narrative used and exploited by black people in our everyday grapplings with "the world and [our] place in it." That "its most hegemonic appearances and manifestations have been masculinist and homophobic," notwithstanding, black nationalism is still a powerful organizing tool for black people struggling with and against racist misfortunes, but often dangerously so for its frequent reactionary appeals to disciplining (policing) the borders of blackness. It constantly forecloses the question, "What is blackness?"

4. In 1970, when I had just begun to teach, two young black transvestite men, who were students at Rutgers University's Livingston College, befriended me. Livingston was established in 1969 as a college where radical curricular alternatives were possible. At that time, Nikki Giovanni was an instructor in the Livingston English Department and was teaching various courses on "the Black Experience," as were Toni Cade, Sonia Sanchez, Miguel Algarin, Jayne Cortez, and many other arbiters and exponents of Black and Latino cultural revolutions. These young "queens" were always in extreme drag, always attended all the events for black students, and were involved in the gay movement on campus, at that time under the leadership of a black gay man. One day the three of us were discussing the overbearing nationalism of the campus black student organization and its homophobia. One of the "queens," who was in Giovanni's class, started to recite her poem, "A Poem Because," as an authoritative reference for tolerance. "They ought to read Nikki on this thing, girl. She sets the record straight," one of the queens asserted to the other. Since that time I have always held onto this poem and that moment, thirty years ago, as evidence of possibility.

5. Black feminist critics and theorists have contributed mightily to the study of black women writers in the last twenty years. The 1980s was a watershed period of black feminist critical production. Truly, many times the criticism is as daring as the literary works themselves. Articles, anthologies, and books that have pushed me are: Akasha (Gloria) Hull, "'Under the Days': The Buried Life and Poetry of Angelina Weld Grimke,"17–47, in *Conditions: Five, the Black*

Women's Issue, 1979; Jewelle L. Gomez, "A Cultural Legacy Denied and Discovered: Black Lesbians in Fiction by Women," 110–123, Gloria Hull, "What It Is I Think She's Doing Anyhow: A Reading of Toni Cadet Barbara's *The Salt Eaters,*"124–144, and Linda C. Powell, "Black Macho and Black Feminism," 283–292, in *Home Girls,* ed. Smith, 1983; Hortense Spillers, "Interstices: A Small Drama of Words," in *Pleasure and Danger,* ed. Carole Vance; June Jordan, *On Call: Political Essays,* 1985; Marjorie Pryse and H. Spillers, eds., *Conjuring: Black Women, Fiction, and Literary Tradition,* 1985; Hazel Carby, *Reconstructing Womanhood: The Emergence of the Afro-American Woman Novelist,* 1987; Mary Helen Washington, "The Darkened Eye Restored: Notes Toward a Literary History of Black Women," in *Invented Lives Narratives of Black Women, 1860–1960,* 1987; Cheryl A. Wall, ed., *Changing Our Own Words: Essays on Criticism, Theory, and Writing by Black Women,* 1989, especially Gloria Hull's and Mae G. Henderson's articles. Also there was response from emerging black feminist critics who were provoked by the thought of lesbianism in our literature. One of the first responses was that of Deborah McDowell in "New Directions for Black Feminist Criticism," originally in *Black Literature Forum* in 1980, in which she questions whether Smith's insistence on "lesbianism," "lesbian literature," "lesbian aesthetic" is not finally "reductive," though she (Smith) "raises critical issues on which black feminist critics can build." Ten years later, McDowell offers a corrective lens to her piece, while still maintaining that Smith's criticism was based on "biology" in "*The Changing Same": Black Women's Literature, Criticism, and Theory* (Bloomington: Indiana University Press, 1995), 16–23. Hazel Carby, while critical of McDowell's loose parameters for black feminist criticism, makes a similar criticism about the biological imperative. That is, Smith's "reliance on common experiences confines black feminist criticism to black women critics of black women artists depicting black women"; see *Reconstructing Womanhood: The Emergence of the Afro-American Woman Novelist* (New York: Oxford University Press, 1987).

6. June Jordan writes about this conference in her book of essays *Civil Wars.* In her introductory remarks, she went out on a limb of her own. She told the audience that she had been raped during the previous fall and, on that very basis, understood why she needed feminism. Howard's Cramton Auditorium, which held at least five hundred people, was filled to capacity. Audre Lorde was in the audience, along with seven or eight other black lesbians, including me, who had come to see and support Smith and Jordan.

The emphatic hostility astounded both Smith and Jordan. In the midst of the lecture Jordan and Smith continued to field all the questions, comments, sermons, and rantings. Many people stayed to talk and argue through the vexed questions of sexuality—and lesbian identity—with Smith, Jordan, and Smith's lesbian support-ers. In his remarks at the closing, Henderson made a personal state-ment symmetrical to Jordan's. Henderson, who was editor of the 1972 volume *Understanding the New Black Poetry*, stated that he wished his wife, who was in a wheelchair, could have attended the workshop.

7. The Stonewall Rebellion of 1969 occurred in this mostly gay bar/club on June 25, 1969. Often harassed by New York's Finest, patrons of the Stonewall fought back over a three-day period, by barricading themselves inside, and throwing bottles and other ob-jects at police as they arrested various demonstrators on the outside, many of whom were black and Latino transvestites, who proved that they were just as "manly" as any policeman. Unheard of within the gay community and certainly not the tactic taken by the pre-Stonewall homosexual rights organizations like Mattachine and Daughters of Bilitis, this three-day riot in New York's Greenwich Village, historic haven for homosexual women and men, ignited al-most overnight the gay and lesbian liberation movement. Stonewall is a fixed marker in the development of gay and lesbian activism in the United States.

8. Rich won and insisted upon sharing the award with her sister fem-inists, Walker and Lorde, rejecting the American custom of "canon-izing" its writers and thereby isolating them from their constituents. On the cover of subsequent editions of *Diving*, Rich also insisted that its cover read: "Co-winner of the 1974 National Book Award."

9. Lorde proclaimed her prose work, *Zami: A New Spelling of My Name* (1983), to be a biomythography, a narrative whose author uses some autobiographical material in the writing, which is also infused with fictive qualities. I am calling Dahomey Lorde's (bio)mythographical home in a similar sense, in that she constructs an imagined African source of black lesbian creativity in the United States.

10. Assata Shakur, also known as Joanne Chesimard, is a political activist and black revolutionary woman who escaped from Clinton Prison (New Jersey) in 1978 to Cuba and was given political asylum.

11. Elly Bulkin, Irena Klepfisz, Rima Shore, and Jan Clausen founded *Conditions* as "a magazine of writing by women with an emphasis on writing by lesbians" in 1976 and published the first issue in 1977. *Conditions* closed its pages in 1990 because of flagging re-sources and editorial energy. During its years of publication, it be-came a repository of the multicultural lesbian literary culture. Its contributors included Paula Gunn Allen, Dorothy Allison, Gloria Anzaldua, Jewelle Gomez, Judy Grahn, Joy Harjo, Audre Lorde, Cherríe Moraga, Minnie Bruce Pratt, Adrienne Rich, Sapphire, Shay Youngblood as well as Barbara Smith and myself. *Conditions: Five*, however, caused the editors to rethink their commitments to lesbian communities. Not only must black women and other

women of color see themselves on the pages of so-called lesbian publications, but they must also be involved in the decisions that produce those publications. In 1981, the editors recruited an eight-person collective, which included three African-American women, one white working-class woman, one Latina, two Jewish women, and one White Anglo-Saxon Protestant lesbian. Successive collectives remained committed to this model as well as to each member's requisite lesbianism. I was a member of the collective from 1981 to 1990.

12. *This Bridge Called My Back: Writings By Radical Women of Color* was originally published by Persephone Press, an independent women's press in Watertown, Mass., which folded circa 1982. In 1983, Kitchen Table published and continued to publish *This Bridge* until the late 1990s. Persephone Press was quite active while it lasted and it published several other key lesbian-feminist texts, *Nice Jewish Girls*, edited by Evelynn Torton Beck, *Lesbian Poetry*, edited by Elly Bulkin and Joan Larkin in 1981, and *Lesbian Fiction*, also edited by Bulkin in 1981.

WORKS CITED

Baker, Houston A. Jr., *Modernism and the Harlem Renaissance*. Chicago: University of Chicago Press. 1987.

———. "Generational Shifts and the Recent Criticism of Afro-American Literature" (1981). In *Within the Circle*, ed. Angelyn Mitchell, Durham, N.C.: Duke University Press, 1994. 282–328.

———. *Workings of the Spirit: The Poetics Of Afro-American Women Writing*. With a Phototext by Elizabeth Alexander and Patricia Redmond. Chicago: University of Chicago Press, 1991.

Bambara, Toni Cade. *The Black Women*. New York: New American Library, 1970.

Baraka, Amiri. *The Autobiography of LeRoi Jones*. Chicago: Lawrence Hill Books, 1997.

———. "Black Woman." *Raise Race Rays Raze: Essays Since 1965*. New York: Random House, 1971. 147–154.

———. "The Changing Same: R&B and New Black Music" [1966]. *Black Music*. New York: Da Capo Press, 1998. 180–212.

———. *Eulogies*. New York: Marsilio Publishers, 1996.

———. "Rhythm and Blues," "Black Dada Nihilismus." In *The Dead Lecturer*. New York: Grove Press, 1964.

———. "Speech to the Congress of African People" (1970). In *Modern Black Nationalism: From Marcus Garvey to Louis Farrakhan*, ed. William L. Van Deburg. New York: New York University Press, 1997. 145–157.

———. (LeRoi Jones). "State/meant." In *Home: Social Essays*. New York: William Morrow, 1966. 251–252.

———. *Transbluesency: The Selected Poems of Amiri Baraka/LeRoi Jones* (1961–1995). Ed. Paul Vangelisti. New York: Marsilio Publishers, 1995.

Blount, Marcellus: "Caged Birds: Race and Gender in the Sonnet." In *Engendering Men: The Question of Male Feminist Criticism*, ed. Joseph A. Boone and Michael Cadden. New York: Routledge, 1990.

Bonetti, Kay. Interviewer. "An Interview with Ntozake Shange." Rec. 1989. *American Audio Prose Library Presents*. Audiotape. Columbia, Mo.: AAPL, 1989.

Brooks, Gwendolyn. ed. *A Broadside Treasury.* Detroit, Mich.: Broadside Press, 1971.

———. *In The Mecca.* New York: Harper and Row, 1968.

———. *Report From Part One.* 1972. Detroit, Mich.: Broadside Press, 1991.

———. *Riot.* Detroit, Mich.: Broadside Press, 1969.

Brown, Fahamisha Patricia. *Performing the Word: African American Poetry as Vernacular Culture.* New Brunswick, N.J.: Rutgers University Press, 1999.

Brown, Sterling. "Ma Rainey." *The Collected Poems of Sterling Brown,* ed. Michael Harper. Chicago: TriQuarterly Books, 1989.

Carson, Claybourne. *SNCC And The Black Awakening Of The 1960's.* 1981; Cambridge: Harvard University Press, 1995.

Chinasole. "Audre Lorde and Matrilineal Diaspora: 'moving history beyond nightmare into structures for the future'." In *Wild Women in the Whirlwind: Afra-American Culture and the Contemporary Literary Renaissance,* ed. Joanne Braxton and Andree N. McLaughlin. New Brunswick, N.J: Rutgers University Press, 1990. 379–394.

Clausen, Jan. *A Movement of Poets.* Brooklyn, N.Y.: Long Haul Press, 1982.

Clifton, Lucille. *Generations: A Memoir.* New York: Random House, 1976.

———. *Good Woman: Poems and a Memoir. 1969–1980.* Brockport, N.Y.: BOA Editions, Ltd., 1987.

———. *The Terrible Stories: Poems.* Brockport, N.Y.: BOA Editions, Ltd., 1997.

Combahee River Collective. "A Black Feminist Statement" (1977). In *Home Girls: A Black Feminist Anthology,* ed. Barbara Smith. New Brunswick, N.J.: Rutgers University Press, 2000.

Cortez, Jayne. *Pisstained Stairs and the Monkey Man's Wares.* Self-published manuscript, 1969. Schomburg Center for African-American Culture, New York City.

———. *Scarifications.* 1973; New York: Bola Press, 1978.

Damon, Maria. *the Dark End of the Street: Margins in American Vanguard Poetry.* Minneapolis: University of Minnesota Press, 1993.

Davis, Angela. "Reflections On The Black Woman's Role In The Community of Slaves." *The Black Scholar* (December 1971): 3–15.

Douglass, Frederick. *Narrative of the Life of Frederick Douglass, an American Slave, Written by Himself.* 1845. In *The Classic Slave Narratives,* ed. Henry Louis Gates, Jr. New York: New American Library, 1987.

Drake, St. Claire, and Horace Cayton. *Black Metropolis: A Study of Negro Life In A Northern City.* Chicago: University of Chicago Press, 1970.

Felman, Shoshana, and Dori Laub, M.D. *Testimony: Crises of Witnessing in Literature, Psychoanalysis, and History.* New York: Routledge, 1992.

Franklin, Aretha. "The Thrill Is Gone." By Art Benson/Dale Petite. Rec. 24 August 1970. *Aretha Franklin: Spirit in the Dark*. Atlantic, 1993.

French, William P., Michael Fabre, and Amritjit Singh, eds. *Afro-American Poetry and Drama. 1760–1975*. Detroit: Gale Research Co., 1979.

Fuller, Hoyt. "Towards a Black Aesthetic" (1968). In *Within The Circle*, ed. Angelyn Mitchell. Durham, N.C.: Duke University Press, 1994. 199–206.

Gates, Henry Louis Jr. "Melvin B. Tolson (1900?–1966)." Eds. Henry Louis Gates, Jr. and Nellie Y. McKay. *The Norton Anthology of African-American Literature*. New York: Norton, 1997.

———. *Signifyin(g) Monkey: The Theory of African-American Criticism*. Oxford: Oxford University Press, 1988.

———. *Figures in Black: Words, Signs, and the "Racial" Self*. New York: Oxford University Press, 1988.

Giovanni, Nikki. *Black Feeling Black Talk Black Judgment*. New York: William Morrow & Co., 1970.

———. *Black Judgment*. Detroit, Mich.: Broadside Press, 1971.

———. "Black Poems, Poseurs and Power." *Gemini: An Extended Autobiographical Statement on My First Twenty-Five Years of Being a Black Poet*. New York: Penguin Books, 1971.

———. "Poem for Aretha." Ed. Gwendolyn Brooks. *Broadside Treasury*. Detroit, Mi.: Broadside Press, 1970.

———. *re creation*. Detroit, Mich.: Broadside Press, 1970.

———. *This Is My House*. New York: William Morrow. 1972.

Greenberg, Cheryl Lynn, ed. *A Circle of Trust: Remembering SNCC*. New Brunswick, N.J.: Rutgers University Press, 1998.

Harper, Phillip Brian. *Are We Not Men?: Masculine Anxiety and the Problem of African-American Identity*. New York: Oxford University Press, 1996.

Heacock, Maureen Catherine. "Sounding a Challenge: African American Women's Poetry and the Black Arts Movement." Ph.D. diss, University of Minnesota, 1996.

Henderson, Stephen. "Introduction: The Forms of Things Unknown." In *Understanding the New Black Poetry: Black Speech and Black Music as Poetic References*, ed. Henderson. New York: William Morrow, 1973.

Holloway, Karla F. C. *Moorings & Metaphors: Figures of Culture in Black Women's Literature*. New Brunswick, N.J.: Rutgers University Press, 1992.

Hull, Gloria T. "Living on the Line: Audre Lorde and *Our Dead Behind Us*." *Changing Our Own Words: Essays on Criticism, Theory, and Writing by Black Women*, ed. Cheryl Wall. New Brunswick, N.J.: Rutgers University Press, 1989. 151–172.

Jefferson, Thomas. *Notes on the State of Virginia*. Ed. William Peden. New York: W. W. Norton & Company, 1982.

Jordan, June. *Things that I Do In The Dark*. New York: Random House, 1977.

Keating, AnaLouise. *Women Reading Women Writing: Self-Invention in Paula Gunn Allen, Gloria Anzaldua, and Audre Lorde*. Philadelphia: Temple University Press, 1996.

Lee, Don L. "blackwoman." In *A Broadside Treasury*, ed. Gwendolyn Brooks. Detroit, Mich.: Broadside Press, 1971.

———. *We Walk The Way of The New World*. Detroit, Mich.: Broadside Press, 1970.

Lester, Neal A. *Ntozake Shange: A Critical Study of the Plays*. New York: Garland Publishing, 1995.

———. "Shange's Men: For Colored Girls Revisited, and Movement Beyond." *African American Review* 26, 2 (1992):.

Levine, Lawrence. *Black Culture and Black Consciousness: Afro-American Folk Thought From Slavery to Freedom*. New York: Penguin Books, 1977.

Lindsey, Kay. "Poem." In *The Black Woman: An Anthology*, ed. Toni Cade (Bambara). New York: New American Library, 1970. 17.

Lofton, Elouise. *Jumbish*. New York: Emerson Hall Publications, 1972.

Lorde, Audre. *Black Unicorn*. New York: Norton, 1978.

———. *A Burst of Light*. Ithaca, N.Y.: Firebrand Books, 1988.

———. From a Land Where Other People Live. Detroit, Mich.: Broadside Press, 1973.

———. *Sister Outsider: Essays and Speeches*. Freedom, Calif.: The Crossing Press (Feminist Series), 1984.

———. *Undersong: Chosen Poems. Old and New*. Revised. New York: W.W. Norton, 1992.

Lubiano, Wahneema. "Black Nationalism and Black Common Sense: Policing Ourselves and Others." In *The House That Race Built: Black Americans, U.S. Terrain*, ed. Wahneema Lubiano. New York: Pantheon Books, 1997. 232–252.

Madhubuti, Haki. "Toward a Definition: Black Poetry of the Sixties (After LeRoi Jones)." In *Within the Circle*, ed. Angelyn Mitchell. Durham: Duke University Press, 1994. 213–223.

Major, Clarence, ed. *The New Black Poetry*. New York: International Publishers, 1969.

McDowell, Deborah E. *The Changing Same: Black Women's Literature. Criticism. and Theory*. Bloomington: Indiana University Press, 1995.

Melhem, D. H. *Gwendolyn Brooks: Poetry and the Heroic Voice*. Lexington: University of Kentucky Press, 1987.

Morris, Tracie. *Intermission*. Brooklyn, N.Y.: Soft Skull Press, 1998.

Nathan, David. "Liner notes." *Aretha Franklin: Spirit in the Dark*. CD. Atlantic Recording Corp., 1970, 1993.

Nielsen, Aldon Lynn. *Black Chant: Languages of African-American Postmodernism*. New York: Cambridge University Press, 1997.

Novak, Phillip. "'Circles and Circles of Sorrow': In the Wake of Morrison's Sula." *PMLA* 114 (1999): 184–193.

Parker, Pat. *Movement in Black*. 1978, Ithaca, N.Y.: Firebrand Books, 1989. 37.

———. "Where Will You Be." *Conditions: Five. The Black Women's Issue* (1979): 128–132.

Ramazani, Jahan. *Poetry of Mourning: The Modern Elegy From Hardy to Heaney*. Chicago: University of Chicago Press, 1994.

Rodgers, Carolyn. *how i got ovah*. Garden City, N.Y.: Anchor Press/Doubleday, 1976.

Rose, Tricia. *Black Noise: Rap Music and Black Culture in Contemporary America*. Hanover, N.H.: Wesleyan University Press, 1994.

Sanchez, Sonia. "so this is our revolution." In *Broadside Treasury*, ed. Gwendolyn Brooks. Detroit, Mich.: Broadside Press, 1970. 144.

———. *We A BaddDDD People*. Detroit, Mich.: Broadside Press, 1970.

Shange, Ntozake. *For Colored Girls Who Have Considered Suicide When The Rainbow Is Enuf*. San Francisco: Shameless Hussy Press, 1975.

———. *for colored girls who have considered suicide when the rainbow is enuf: a choreopoem*. New York: Collier-MacMillan Company, 1977.

———. "Program Note." (1981) *See No Evil: Prefaces, Essays & Accounts, 1976–1983*. San Francisco: Momo's Press, 1984.

———. "things i wd say." In *nappy edges*. New York: St. Martin's Press, 1978.

Simmons, Judy D. *Judith's Blues*. Detroit, Mich.: Broadside Press, 1973. 10.

Smith, Barbara. "Towards a Black Feminist Criticism." *Conditions: Two* (October 1977): 25–52.

Smith, Barbara, and Lorraine Bethel, guest eds. *Conditions: Five, The Black Women's Issue* 2, no. 2 (1979): 12.

Smith, David Lionel. "The Black Arts Movement and Its Critics." *American Literary History* 3 (Spring 1991): 93–110.

Spillers, Hortense J. "Gwendolyn the Terrible: Propositions on Eleven Poems," "'An Order of Constancy': Notes on Brooks and the Feminine." In *Black, White, and in Color: Esays on American Literature and Culture*. Chicago: University of Chicago Press, 2003.

Splawn, P. Jane. "'Change the Joke[r] and slip the yoke': Boal's 'Joker' system in Ntozake Shange's *for colored girls* and *spell #7*." *Modern Drama* 41, no. 3 386–398.

Staples, Robert. "The Myth of Black Macho: A Response to Angry Black Feminists." *The Black Scholar* (March/April 1979): 24–36.

Student Nonviolent Coordinating Committee. "Position Paper on Black Power." 1966. *Modern Black Nationalism: From Marcus Garvey to Louis*

Farrakhan, ed. William L. Van Deburg. New York: New York University Press, 1997. 122.

Tate, Claudia. *Black Women Writers at Work: Conversations with*. New York: Continuum Publishing Company, 1983.

Taylor, Henry. "Gwendolyn Brooks: An Essential Sanity." *Kenyon Review* 13, 4 (1991): 115–131.

Van Deburg, William L. *Modern Black Nationalism: From Marcus Garvey to Louis Farrakhan*. 1997.

———. *New Day in Babylon: The Black Power Movement and American Culture. 1965–1975*. New York: New York University Press, 1992.

Walker, Alice. "In Search of Our Mothers' Gardens." *In Search of Our Mother's Gardens: Womanist Prose*. New York: Harcourt, 1983.

———. *Once. Her Blue Body Everything We Know: Earthling Poems 1965–1990 Complete*. San Diego, New York, London: A Harvest Book, 1991.

———. *Revolutionary Petunias*. New York: Harcourt Brace Jovanovich, 1973.

Wall, Cheryl, ed. *Changing Our Own Words: Essays on Criticism. Theory and Writing by Black Women*. New Brunswick, N.J.: Rutgers University Press, 1989.

Wallace, Michele. *Black Macho and the Myth of the Superwoman*. New York: Dial Press, 1978.

Washington, James M., ed. *A Testament of Hope: The Essential Writings and Speeches of Martin Luther King Jr*. New York: HarperSanFrancisco, 1986.

Washington, Mary Helen. "Introduction: A Woman Half In Shadow." In *I Love Myself When I Am Laughing . . . And Then Again When I Am Looking Mean and Impressive: A Zora Neale Hurston Reader*, ed. Alice Walker. Old Westbury, N.Y.: Feminist Press, 1979.

Williams, Kenny J. "Restricted Chicago of Gwendolyn Brooks." In *A Life Distilled: Gwendolyn Brooks, Her Poetry and Fiction*, ed. Maria K. Mootry and Gary Smith. Urbana: University of Illinois Press, 1987. 47–70.

Index

Permissions

About the Author

Cheryl Lynn Clarke is the director of Diverse Community Affairs and LGBT concerns at Rutgers University. She is the author of four books of poetry, *Narratives: poems in the tradition of black women* (Kitchen Table/Women of Color, 1983), *Living as a Lesbian* (Firebrand Books, 1986), *Humid Pitch* (Firebrand Books, 1989), and *Experimental Love* (Firebrand Books, 1993).